# Second Opinion

## Taking the Bite Out of Dentistry

by Dan L. Watt D.D.S

The views expressed in this book are those of the author and not necessarily those of the International Dental Health Foundation or its members.

ISBN 0-9612862-8-8

# TABLE OF CONTENTS

## PART ONE

### DENTAL DISEASES AND THE DENTAL PROFESSION

## PART TWO

### A PATIENT'S GUIDE TO DENTAL HEALTH

"Tis my want of a morning to rub my teeth with salt, and then swill my mouth out with water: and often after eating, to clean my back teeth with a toothpick, as well as rubbing them hard with a cloth: wherefore my teeth, back and front, remain as clean and white as falleth to the lot of few men of my years, and my gums (no matter how hard the salt be that I rub them with) never start bleeding. Yet notwithstanding, my teeth are not so clean thereby, but what there sticketh or groweth between some of my front ones and my grinders (whenever I inspected them with a magnifying mirror), a little white matter, which is as thick, as if 'twere batter. On examining, this, I judged (albeit I could discern nought a-moving in it) that there yet were living animalcules therein."

Anthony Von Leeuwenhoek
September 17, 1683

# FOREWORD

Dear Reader:

In August, 1986, a dentist informed me that I had periodontal disease which would require me to seek the services of a periodontist in order to save my teeth. As a preliminary measure, I made an appointment with another dentist to obtain a second opinion. He confirmed the diagnosis and referred me to a periodontist.

Following the dental examination, the periodontist provided me with a treatment plan, including surgery in order to perform a deep root scaling and planing to remove plaque which had built-up below the gumline. In addition, he informed me that my four upper front teeth would require capping to mask the impending disfiguration resulting from the surgery. He anticipated a total treatment cost of between $10,000 to $12,000. He also cautioned me that without surgery I would surely lose my teeth. It is also important to mention that he indicated that the surgery would not be a permanent resolution to the disease and a recurrence of the disease could occur in five to seven years. Therefore, he could not provide me with a guarantee. No other alternative treatment plan was offered albeit dentures.

To say the least, I was devastated, not only with the thought of losing my teeth, but with the exorbitant cost of the treatment. I was not in the financial position to afford $10,000, and at age forty-one I began seriously to consider resigning myself to life with a set of dentures.

Since my teens I have enjoyed the **Reader's Digest** magazine. On this occasion, the magazine provided me with a most needed alternative to my dental problem. In its October, 1986, issue, an article entitled *Do These Dentists Do Too Much* summarized research conducted by Dr. Paul H. Keyes in the successful treatment of periodontal diseases *without surgery.* The article also stated that prior to Dr. Keyes' retirement he was affiliated with the National Institutes of Health (NIH) near Washington, D.C. Now I knew there was an alternative to my problem and I set about obtaining more information. I called NIH in an attempt to reach Dr. Keyes. They were very helpful and informed me that although Dr. Keyes was no longer practicing, his colleague, Dr. Dan L. Watt was carrying on the research in conjunction with a busy dental practice in Reston, Virginia. Needless to say, I contacted Dr. Watt immediately.

It is now one and a half years later and I still have my teeth. My four front teeth are also still my own with no caps, and I am continuing with Dr. Watt's treatment as set forth in this book. The total cost of treatment was about $800 which included not only the treatment of the periodontal disease, but some ordinary dental maintenance.

As an aside to my particular experience, I have

also recommended several people to seek Dr. Watt's treatment as an alternative to surgery. Each and everyone of them has been pleased with the results and have gratefully avoided a very painful and disfiguring procedure as generally made available to them by the periodontal profession.

My statements in no way presume that the periodontal profession is without merit, only that perhaps they are not as progressive as they should be in seeking out new techniques. This holds especially true when it has been proven through research and treatment that an alternative to surgery exists with the same success rate.

Sincerely,

Audrey L. Johns

# ABOUT THE AUTHOR

Dr. Dan L. Watt is a general dentist with a private practice in Reston, Virginia. In 1981 he and Dr. Paul H. Keyes founded the International Dental Health Foundation, a non-profit organization devoted to educating the dental profession and the lay public about a disease management system to aid in the prevention and treatment of periodontal diseases. Since establishing IDHF, Dr. Watt has lectured throughout the United States and in Canada and Mexico on his conservative method of treatment.

A native of Marion, Ohio, his dental school training was received at Ohio State University following an undergraduate major in Microbiology. Upon graduation, the Navy awarded him an internship at Portsmouth Naval Hospital in Virginia. His naval career continued aboard the USS VALLEY FORGE homeported in Long Beach, California, and deployed for a tour of duty off the coast of Vietnam where the ship served as a hospital ship for the Marines. Here, he performed many complex surgical procedures, including wounds to the face. Although a surgical career was contemplated, Dr. Watt decided to enter private general practice.

Discharged in 1970, he entered private practice in Dayton, Ohio. He taught oral surgery and peridontal surgery in the Dental Internship program at Miami Valley Hospital. Two years later, he formed a group practice with two former Navy dentists in Reston, Virginia.

In 1978 he was introduced to the scientific work of Dr. Paul Keyes at the National Institutes of Health in Bethesda, Maryland, and realized that the visions of this researcher were on the right track to understanding, eliminating, and preventing dental diseases. Dr. Watt incorporated Dr. Keyes' findings into his own practice and began to realize phenomenal success in managing gum diseases without painful surgical procedures. He encouraged Dr. Keyes to present his research work to the dental profession. Together they formed the International Dental Health Foundation and developed the Seven Step Treatment System.

Dr. Watt continues to serve as the Chairman of the Board of Trustees of the Foundation and presents approximately twenty to thirty lectures a year throughout the United States. He also remains active in the Naval Reserves, the Academy of General Dentists, and various civic groups within the community of Reston, where he resides with his wife, son, and daughter.

# ACKNOWLEDGMENT

SECOND OPINION is about diseases that infect almost everyone. Because they do not cause pain until the later stages and generally are not considered life threatening, they are tolerated as a costly nuisance. They are so costly that they even have their own separate insurance plans and are treated by a profession that boasts six specialties and numerous subspecialties. Only cancer, heart disease and accidents cost the American public more.

Yet, these diseases are caused by simple microbes that are eliminated by many readily available antibacterial agents. If such agents were employed regularly, the incidence of the diseases would be rare instead of commonplace.

The profession charged with treatment seems content to offer expensive repairs for the damage caused by the diseases and contends that the high incidence of infection is due to a lack of effort by those inflicted to perform proper preventive techniques with such "sophisticated" disease fighting tools as strings and brushes.

Research has provided far more effective tools and treatment procedures, but, since the treating professionals are content (or consumed) with repair, they will maintain the status quo until the public *demands* change.

SECOND OPINION tells all about these microbial infections and the ways they can be eliminated, plus insights into why the treating profession has not been effective in managing these diseases.

Best of all, readers will learn how to save themselves, their families and future generations from the ravages of these infections.

I know that anyone who assimulates the information within these pages will have the opportunity to be healthier. That is my mission and reason for writing this book.

There are several people that have touched me over the years and made this book a reality. Paul Keyes is certainly one of those who deserves my gratitude for sharing his theories and insights as we traveled together throughout the country presenting seminars to the dental profession. Pat Cartwright, the Foundation's Executive Director, is another individual whose honor, loyalty, sincerity, devotion, and commitment have kept me going when it seemed hopeless to do so. The numerous Foundation member dentists and hygienists, whose undying support have given me the strength to tackle the seemingly insurmountable obstacles placed in our path. And a special thanks is offered to my wife, Barbara, and children, Daniel and Haley, who have had to put up with their father missing soccer games, etc. and traveling when it seemed he was chasing rainbows.

Others that have helped me clarify my thoughts in writing the book: Herman Sturm, C.C. Rosenfelder, Dr. Russell Tontz, Mary Allen White, Pam Cloer, Dr. Ed Grace, etc. There are many others that have enriched my life and kept my mission in focus, GOD BLESS YOU ALL.

# TESTIMONIALS

Dear Reader;

The summer of 1987 I left on vacation with a gum infection. My dentist had started me on penicillin. While on the penicillin I developed a second gum infection which caused a tooth to become very loose. I contacted my dentist immediately on returning and he sent me to a periodontist.

The periodontist saw me within a day, examined me and concluded that I needed five teeth removed. He also scolded me for not flossing my teeth better! I felt somewhat humiliated, went back to my original dentist and sought a second opinion. This time I saw another periodontist who worked in a huge suite in a Washington highrise, and who collaborated with another dentist. They took a full set of x-rays and concluded that I needed massive gum surgery, 15 teeth removed, implants and probably bone grafts. The estimated cost was over $10,000.

How did I get into this mess! I had been seeing my original dentist regularly for at least fifteen years and he seemed like a thoughtful, caring, and competent individual. He was familiar with modern notions of treatment of gum disease and elimination of plaque. I regularly brushed with baking soda and hydrogen peroxide, water picked with a salt water solution every other night, and now I was being told that I needed half of the teeth in my mouth *removed!*

I am one of those individuals who under stress tends to get gum infections. When my resistence is low my mouth is my place of vulnerability. My dentist and I knew this and so I carried a prescription for penicillin and would immediately start on it at the first sign of infection. Both my dentist and I thought we were dealing with my gum infection problems.

I became determined to avoid this massive assault on my mouth and contacted the International Dental Health Foundation who referred me to Dr. Watt. He took samples from between my teeth and showed me the active infection that was untouched by penicillin. He started me on a regimen that included scaling deeply into my gum pockets (many of which were about a half inch deep) and using an irrigation system that delivered powerful germicides deep into these gum pockets. This is something I do at home with a specially adapted mouth irrigator. Dr. Watt continues to monitor the bacterial level in my gums and we make small adjustments in technique as needed.

The result is that I have *lost no teeth!* All the deep pockets in my mouth have become more shallow and the tooth that was most loose has become stable, although I did have one additional infection where I evidently was not reaching a pocket on my last molar. This infection was quickly cleared up.

I feel a mixture of both anger and relief. Anger at the seemingly irresponsible way I had been treated by two periodontists, and relief to have found a method that not only is rational, but that is clearly effective at nominal costs.

Try to imagine having an infected puncture wound that is half an inch deep on any other part of your body, and being told that adequate and proper care of that infected wound is to wash the surface once a day with soapy water. That would be absurd. Yet so called "modern dentistry" treats similar infections in essentially such a manner. Clearly there is no way brushing, flossing, or mouth rinsing could affect the infection in these deep pockets. No attempt was made to check to see if the bacteria involved were sensitive to penicillin and, since it only seemed to reduce the acute symptoms, was it really helping much at all? What is necessary is to identify the offending bacteria, find out what kills them and make sure the antibacterial agents reach every nook and cranny where the bacteria thrive. This is the way to eradicate an infection and that is what Dr. Watt has helped me to do.

So, at age 55, I have learned my lessons and learned them the hard way. I hope my experiences will help you.

Sincerely,

Lawrence Tirnauer

Dear Dan and Staff,

The three day meeting that was condensed into two days and one evening this past weekend was a very successful "experiment" as far as I can tell. Thank you!

My staff and I feel like we are now more qualified to update and modify our current preventive and therapy programs using our new knowledge of oral microbiology that you and your team shared with us so unselfishly. Not only were the presentations factual and unbiased, they were sufficiently motivating to "put us in action" so that we now have both the knowledge and the desire to serve our patients much more effectively.

More importantly, perhaps, I personally have a sense of excitement and a much deeper respect and admiration of the dental profession for having "decoded" periodontal disease for the first time in the history of mankind. I see this as a true breakthough for the human race, allowing all of us a much higher quality of life not available until now. There is no doubt this new attitude toward the value of our day to day contribution to our patients' well-being will go a long way toward personal fulfillment in our work, thereby avoiding or minimizing the dental "burnout" syndrome so prevalent in our profession.

Consequently, I want you and your team to fully understand that you aren't just teaching a new effective way to treat periodontal disease, but, in reality, you are making a *profound difference* in the way that dentists, dental staff people and dental patients feel about dentistry and dental health. This obviously includes, or will soon include, every person on our planet. It does not take a lot of imagination to see that the ability of a person to maintain a healthy, functional mouth for a lifetime will certainly contribute to the quality of his life in an enormously positive way.

The purpose of this letter is to specifically thank Dr. Paul Keyes, you, your staff and all the other people who have made this breakthrough happen. It is my sincere hope that you can forgive those individuals who, through understandable ignorance, have been unduly critical of your work.

In my opinion, the results of your work now speak for themselves and the original criticism is now being replaced with enlightenment, appreciation and gratitude. I, for one, hope that you all can take the necessary time, step back for a minute, and enjoy your success to the fullest extent possible!

Dan, please do me a personal favor and share this letter and these intimate thoughts with your friends and colleagues who have labored on this long-term project with you, especially Dr. Paul Keyes. The vision, original research, implementation and communication of this work to the profession and to the public will surely serve as an inspiration to many of us for a long time to come.

Once again, thank all of you for your contribution to me and to the human race. It is indeed a distinct honor to know you all personally and to be associated with people like you who are committed to making a difference in the quality of life for all of of us.

Sincerely,

Edward W. Strother, D.M.D.

# PART ONE

# DENTAL DISEASES
# AND THE
# DENTAL PROFESSION

# Chapter 1
# A DIFFERENT VIEW

"Look Mom, no cavities!" This brilliantly conceived television commercial for Proctor & Gamble's new product, Crest, was as popular in the 1960's as Lite Beer commercials are today. People were saying: "My my, look at the progress! Now we don't have any more cavities. It is really nice that those dentists are working themselves out of a job."

The fact that dentists were now viewed as "nice guys" was a far cry from earlier perceptions when just the mention of the word "dentist" struck fear into one's heart. Visions of being strapped into a dental chair and inflicted with horrendous pain were considered normal. Almost everyone has horror stories to tell about themselves or relatives. One such classic story revolved around the old, belt-driven drill with its frayed belt that went thump, thump, thump everytime the frayed end came through the handpiece. Smoke rolled off the tooth from the drill and the patient moaned in agony pleading with the dentist to stop, but the dentist kept on drilling, saying "just a little longer."

Then there are stories about dentists advising their patients that novocaine was not necessary because "this is just a small cavity." But once the drilling started, the drill bit would fall into a deep cavity causing excruciating pain.

1

But in the late 1950's dentistry began to change. A Navy dentist by the name of Borden invented a new air drill that went 250,000 revolutions per minute. Cutting through tough tooth enamel was now almost as easy as a knife cutting through butter. Drilling proceeded more quickly and since the drill was cooled by a water spray, pain was greatly diminished.

Disposable needles had also been developed. Needles were no longer used and re-used to the point of being dull and painful. New local anesthetics were available and more anesthesia was being administered.

These advancements, along with improved techniques such as life-like crowns and bonded tooth-colored filling materials, put dentistry in a more positive light. Dentists were also becoming aware of behavioral psychology and they used this beneficial knowledge to overcome their "bad guy" image. Dentists were jet propelled to unheard of levels of respect. Public opinion polls showed that dentists had a higher degree of public trust than physicians and other professionals, so it really appeared that dentistry was the only profession truly trying to work itself out of a job. But a more detailed look at the profession, its accomplishments, its shortcomings, and its downright obstinacy will reveal a different picture and make you wonder why it has taken so long to solve the dilemma of dental diseases.

What really is dental disease? A cavity is nothing more than the damage resulting from an infection by bacteria to a hard surface in the body. Periodontal or gum diseases are also caused by an infection of microorganisms which are dominated by bacteria. Dentistry fights these infections primarily with dental floss and toothbrushes with the help of professional cleanings and tools, such as stimulators and wooden picks. Have you ever heard of infections in any other part of the body being treated with such products? Have you noticed that dental infections are among the very few bacterial infections that have not yet been cured?

Wouldn't you feel quite unhappy with your physician if you constantly had to return for treatment of damage caused by a bacterial infection and be told that the reason was your fault because you were not flossing and brushing properly? Wouldn't you want him/ her to find the cause of the problem and eliminate it? Wouldn't you expect him/her to do something in terms of antimicrobial or antibacterial therapy, and wouldn't you be upset if you discovered the bacteria associated with these diseases respond quite well to standard antimicrobial therapy?

If you do not believe that statement, look what happened when fluoride was added in very low dosages to drinking water and toothpastes. Although dentists have received the credit for the lower decay rate, their contribution has had only marginal impact when compared to that of the persons putting the fluoride into the drinking water and toothpastes.

Dentists generally recommend that patients come in every six months for a cleaning and check-up. Would you be surprised to learn that this standard six-month recall system is based on a toothpaste commercial made by the heroes of a famous radio show? Amos said to Andy, "See your dentist every six months and brush your teeth with Pepsodent." This frequent advertisement in the 1930's quickly established the "norm."

Diagnostic systems in dentistry have never been very sophisticated. Cavities are detected by running a sharp probe into the bottom of tooth crevices to detect soft, gummy areas. If the probe stuck, then the tooth needed a filling. X-ray interpretation for cavities varies between dental schools. Some schools are conservative. They teach that a discrepancy in the enamel surface may just be an arrested lesion and need not be filled until the lesion penetrates through the enamel into the dentine of the tooth. Others teach that any defect should be filled. That is why many people have had the experience of going to one dentist who detects five cavities while another dentist finds none. Almost no dentists use tests to determine whether the decay is actively progressing or arrested.

Now all this may seem strange until you realize that dentistry is based on *mechanical thinking*. The emphasis in dental schools is on how tightly your crowns fit, how pretty and well-condensed your fillings are. Even the State Board examination necessary to obtain a license to practice forces aspiring practitioners to perform complicated, but seldom used procedures. A classic example is the gold foil filling that has not been used in private practices for several years because of its difficulty in placement, its cost, and the plain fact that other less complicated fillings are as effective and more cosmetically appealing. But it continues to be a major point on State Board examinations—glowing proof that such obstinate, narrow, mechanical thinking is still quite pervasive today.

Let's not give the dental profession too bad a rap. We had good reason to react the way we did. Since the first dental school was established in Baltimore in 1840, dentists have been overwhelmed with damaged teeth. It has taken all of our energy to find ways to save teeth through sophisticated and complicated repair techniques. It is no wonder that we dentists find ourselves so engrossed in the mechanics of repair that the cause of the disease is not a high priority. Besides, we have been told that the bacteria causing the problems were "normal" oral inhabitants. This means that it is a cleaning problem and, therefore, really the patients' responsibility to provide the bulk of preventive care. We can only supervise. Besides, this thinking allows us to concentrate on the "real" dentistry of repairing teeth.

The Crest "No Cavities" commercial was the beginning of a new era in dentistry and paved the way for the use of other antimicrobial agents that are finally leading us from an overwhelming incidence of disease.

The high incidence of dental disease is no doubt the greatest indictment against fighting these infections with mechanical means alone. The epidemic nature of periodontal (gum) disease was best expressed in several papers. One sponsored by the Kellogg Foundation (1983) surveyed the dental needs for the state of North Carolina. This study found the needs overwhelming and stated that it would take approximately 485,000 manhours to treat all the cases of gum disease in the state if everyone sought treatment at the same time.

It is estimated that by age thirteen, eighty per cent of Americans begin showing evidence of periodontal disease, and by the age of forty, eighty per cent will have suffered loss of supporting bone and/or several teeth. As the "Golden Years" approach, periodontal disease emerges as a major health problem. Even the Black Plague affected less people!

Another paper, the Iowa Survey of Oral Health (1980), leads to even more startling discoveries. Sixty-eight per cent of the people over age eighteen in the state of Iowa required some type of periodontal treatment. Surprisingly, a high proportion of these patients had visited the dentist within six to twelve months of the survey. The investigators were further surprised by the revelation that regular dental visitors had a higher level of gingival (gum) bleeding than those who had not sought treatment for over a year. Hence, the indication that frequent attendance for dental care is not a guarantee against periodontal infection. Since only 2.1 per cent of the general dentist's treatment time is spent on specific periodontal therapy, it is not a great surprise.

It is also not surprising to learn that the cost of dental care is the fourth leading health care expenditure. Only cancer, heart disease, and accidents cost the American public more. In spite of this expense, over two million teeth were lost in this country in 1987 and untold millions around the world.

Should dental disease be such a problem? With what is currently known in dental research, we should be able to eradicate this health menace in a very short period of time, and that is the point of discussion in the remaining chapters.

# Chapter 2
# THE MICROBES IN PERIODONTAL DISEASE

A good starting place is to take a direct look at the cause of gum infections. A disturbing fact is that these infection causing bacteria are catching just like any other infection. The most likely method of transmission is through kissing! Now there is a negative thought. Unfortunately, it is true and since most of us have some form of dental disease, kissing takes on added burdens. Having problems with this one? One of the most common bacteria found in gum disease is a spirochete. These creepy creatures look and move like a snake and after watching them for a while one would swear that they can think. The spirochete is a family of organisms that is transmitted only by wet tissue contact or the bites from ticks and mosquitos. A patient might be misled because his dentist has never mentioned a problem and no symptoms were evident. Sometimes the disease is harbored in a dormant state for years without readily apparent symptoms, but the bacteria can still be washed up into the saliva and transmitted to an unsuspecting person. We believe that the infection is passed from one generation to another through normal family embraces. Not all people are infected equally, some remain carriers and some are totally resistant due to a strong immune system. Unfortunately, today's knowledge does not allow us to determine a person's resistance capabilities.

Our best weapons are early detection and elimination, followed by a maintenance program that will prevent reinfection. These weapons are possible today at a very low cost and can be a standard part of the dental checkup.

A study of the bacteria associated with gum disease can be very exciting and provide insights into other marvelous realms of thinking. Many of us have a hard time visualizing a germ or microbe as they are so small that only those with access to a certain type of high-quality microscope have actually seen them. We tend to think of them more as mindless bags of chemicals with a haphazard existence. This is far from the truth and, if we stretch our imagination, we can glean a different impression of this microworld growing next to our teeth.

## The Microbial Ecosystem

Let me take you on a journey into a hidden world deep inside the unseen recesses of your own mouth. Let's begin our journey by pretending to shrink to about one hundred microns. That means we are now only ten times taller than a white blood cell or a small spirochete and smaller than a period at the end of a sentence. If we were standing on the top ledge of gum tissue near the area between two teeth, we would see some fascinating sights. Beneath our feet the gum tissue cells would appear to be ten to fifteen foot plates (our measurement in feet has been shrunken in the same proportions as our bodies) layered similar to rock formations. The surface of the plates (epithelial cells) is ankle breaking rough. Looking across a two hundred foot wide lake (the gingival fluid), we see the craggy surface of a tooth rising higher and higher like a huge mountain.

The constant movement of the tongue is creating hurricane-like forces and tidal waves of saliva crash around us. Only by tucking ourselves deeper between the teeth can we keep from being swept away. It is easy to see how creatures that swim could be swept into the lake of fluid between the tooth and gum.

We don scuba gear and dive into the pool. Immediately, we notice that the fluid is salty and seems somewhat syrupy, like fruit juice. This comes from the large amount of protein and other matter from disintegrating tissue cells, tissue fluid, and decaying bacteria.

Along the craggy root surface of the tooth we see a formation of nonmoving organisms resembling a three dimensional latticework. The part in the shallow or top area appears to have died and calcified similar to coral formations (which is really calculus or tartar). As we swim deeper, the alive sections of the lattice appear more dense and move with the ebb and flow of fluid like dancing plants tuned to a silent orchestra. The process of calcification slowly diminishes as we go deeper. Small, round bacteria, the size of oranges are sticking to the living lattice framework in appealing patterns that make some sections look like corn cobs and others like heavily-laden fruit trees. Other small bacteria seem attracted to this growth and congregate in great numbers within the mass. This whole living growth seems several feet thick and quite dense and is best described as a *"mat."*

Down deeper, teeming masses of highly motile organisms concentrate along the outer surfaces of the dancing mat. Schools of rods spin and flip about like fish, seemingly with no particular purpose, but the school stays close together as if protecting itself. Large rods, ranging from two to six feet in length, glide about like barracuda on the prowl, and teeming masses of thin spirochetes that best resemble moray eels twist about like corkscrews, in and out of every nook and cranny of the whole living ecosystem. It is almost like viewing a patch of jungle infested with hundreds of thousands of snakes frantically writhing about. On the outer surface, the larger spirochetes (about a foot long) are lined up side by side in a very dense pattern and beat in unison.

We look over toward the gum tissue wall and also see much activity. Basketball-size, white spheres are continuously working their way out of the wall of cells leaving large holes in their wake. Some stretch out and pull themselves toward one another, sticking together as they touch. A white wall of these cells has formed around and just outside the teeming bacterial ecosystem, and there is a definite air of hostility between the bacteria and those white blood cells. If a bacterium strays too close, the white cells appear to stick out part of their bodies and engulf the smaller germ until it is swallowed and digested. Some white cells break away and attempt to enter the bacterial mat, but are repelled by the beating spirochetes. More and more white cells break away and some do manage to penetrate the bacterial barrier. It is obvious that a war is going on! As we watch this phenomenal struggle, several revelations hit us like a super nova; both white cells and bacteria exhibit a sense of intelligence and seem to employ strategies to ensure their own survival. The bacteria seem most formidable where the spirochetes and barracuda like rods are dominant. Their actions confuse and slow the white cells, which cower and form a thicker wall in this area. In other locations the white cells seem to be conducting end runs with large numbers penetrating deep into the bacterial mat. The battle waxes and wanes with both sides taking tremendous losses and the fluid is becoming thick with body parts.

The fluid burns and we realize that many of the bacteria contain toxins that are released when they break up (similar to a gnat rolling around underneath the eyelid). This toxic material is setting off alarm systems in certain white cells and they are telling the body to send out more white soldiers.

The motile bacteria seem to be the real defense system for the bacterial ecosystem. The spirochetes line up side by side and beat in unison which causes a circulation of fluid out of the bacterial mat, freeing the mat of its own toxins and bringing in more nutrients to support a more concentrated number of bacteria. Their beating action physically keeps the white blood cells away. The spirochetes and gliding rods release some type of enzyme that tranquilizes the white cells, and when they appear docile, the spirochetes attack them, ripping into their cell walls until the white cells disintegrate. A truly alarming sight!

Other creatures appear to thrive on all this activity. Large blobs, up to ten feet in diameter, glide through the beating spirochetes. These amoebae seem to enjoy a close association with the spirochetal beating and we wonder if these cells might feed off the waste material coming off the mat. Another creature, the trichomonad, moves around much like a foraging mouse, unconcerned about contacting white cells. Certain orange-size, round bacteria appear to have stronger toxins and they may be responsible for the ecosystem gaining a decided edge in this war.

Our gaze notices a strange, yellow substance coming from the tissue. The white cells seem to pull more tightly together and their cell walls appear to thicken, as if donning armor. The bacteria are not so lucky and thousands are immediately affected by this strange liquid. We identify the substance as an antibiotic. The bacteria are retreating rapidly, with the more motile bacteria diving deeper into the thick bacterial ecosystem. The antibiotic is quite deadly to most of the organisms, and bodies of dead bacteria pile onto one another until the antibiotic can no longer penetrate the deep areas of the bacterial mat.

We swim over to the tissue wall and grab tightly as a giant nozzle (irrigation needle) swings over our heads. Out of the nozzle, a forceful stream of antiseptic is spewing forth creating a violent turbulence. We cling for dear life until the nozzle moves on. The fluid is cloudy with dead parts floating all around us. The

once vital mat of living bacteria appears to be destroy-
ed and the surface of the tooth root can be seen through
tangled debris. There are, however, such thick clumps
of dead material that we are convinced some bacteria
survived deep underneath this matter.

We scurry back to the tissue wall just in time as a
huge metal instrument with a sharp edge fills the
entire pocket (dental scaler) and scrapes away large
quantities of the disarrayed mat. Many tissue cells are
also scraped away and we must hide deeper among the
adhering tissue cells to keep from being swept away.
The fluid is filled with debris and an occasional live
bacterium.

Soon after, the nozzle (irrigation needle) spurting
antiseptic comes sweeping through once again and
remaining particulate matter is scattered in the turbulence. Only by clinging to the deepest parts of the
tooth surface and the tissue walls can we and some
remaining hearty bacteria survive.

We decide it is time to leave this fantasy and swim
back to reality.

Now let's ponder what we have experienced.

You have witnessed what I and several thousand
of my colleagues have discovered over the last ten
years. First of all, periodontal diseases are caused by
specific groups of microorganisms that work together
to form an ecosystem. This ecosystem is similar to a
barrier reef where all creatures contribute to a certain
vitality that makes the ecosystem defensible to outside
forces. In other words, organization adds a new
dimension and the whole is far greater than the sum of
the individual parts. This ability to band together has

been most effective as these gum diseases probably have caused more damage to human tissues than any other infection. Throughout history, the majority of humans have suffered the consequences of this effective ecosystem. But, as with other ecosystems, the balance can be altered relatively easily. Simple mechanical scaling has merit as it breaks up the organized structures, but since the organisms are not killed, they can soon reorganize. By introducing antiseptics into the ecosystem before and after scaling and adding antibiotics when necessary, we can actually kill members of that ecosystem so that it cannot transform into a destructive entity.

It might be best understood by turning to nature and seeing situations where the ecological balance has been disrupted and the entire reef, forest or jungle is affected.

My colleagues and I have been using this "medical approach" to periodontal treatment for over ten years with phenomenal success. We have seen disease stop, tissues heal, and bone regenerate at a far better rate than with any other technique.

Our methods are simply understood. We identify, microscopically, those microorganisms that are associated with disease and use various antimicrobial procedures until we reach our goal of seeing only those microorganisms found in healthy mouths. In deeper gum pockets, we use needles that look like a needle for putting air into a football or soccerball. The needles are round on the end and the antiseptic solutions come out the side about one millimeter from the end. Most times, we can reach into any infected area, but, on rare occasions, surgery of a specific site is helpful. The whole system will be explained in detail later and I do not want to move ahead too quickly. There are some marvelous revelations that are afforded by our observations of this bacterial mat, so please allow me this short diversion to discuss the ramifications of the concept of organization.

# Chapter 3
# THE ESSENCE OF
# THE MICROBIAL MAT

The realization that living things so small could have some semblance of intelligence can be most disturbing. These bacteria were organized into an ecosystem and displayed definite patterns that would have to be defined as **behavior**. But we should not expect the microbial world to be different from the rest of nature. Health researchers will tell you they do not have the foggiest idea why white cells do what they do. Lewis Thomas in his book, **LIVES OF A CELL,** tells us that these cells are so complex in structure we may never learn everything about them. We are probably closer to explaining the origin of the cosmos.

Actually, we are now facing one of the major areas where my philosophy differs from the majority of dental educators. They have dismissed the so-called "Keyes Technique," which originally described the bacteria through phase contrast microscopy, because, "It isn't scientific. Dr. Keyes' National Institutes of Health (NIH) study did not have the proper controls, therefore it is invalid and should not even be considered." These dental educators have stated this with so much conviction that Dr. Keyes' work is rarely listed as a reference in articles written about the microbiology of gum diseases. He has been branded an outcast by many of his research colleagues and granted little credibility.

There exists some validity to their argument. One of our targets is the spirochete and the question is asked, "How can you target spirochetes when certain African tribes have exhibited large numbers of spirochetes without apparent disease?" Critics also add that damage from disease appears to happen in acute episodes of activity and long periods of remission, and there appears to be a rise in certain non-motile bacteria during these episodes. They claim that we cannot accurately identify bacteria or quantify them using a phase contrast microscope, therefore it is useless.

It is hoped that a conscientious observer would at least examine the following possibilities.

Almost all dental research today falls into the classical patterns of scientific thinking laid down years ago by the likes of Galileo, Newton, Democritus and others. These men believed that all structures and forms in the world are merely different arrangements of atoms. In other words, the universe is a machine in which each component atom moves entirely under the action of blind forces produced by its neighbors. This was in direct opposition to the views presented by the great Greek philosopher, Aristotle. He proposed that objects and systems subordinate their behavior to an overall plan or destiny. He claimed this to be especially apparent in living systems where all the parts function in a cooperative way to achieve a final purpose. He regarded the universe as a sort of giant organism. This concept, called **teleology**, found its way into Christian theology and forms the basis for Western religious thought, representing God's grand design for the universe.

In 1687, Newton published his work, **Principia,** which described three basic laws of motion that govern material bodies. This epic work has been expanded upon by many physicists, and a perception has evolved that the entire cosmos is reduced to a gigantic clockwork mechanism with each component unfailingly executing its preprogrammed instructions to mathematical precision.

This Newtonian paradigm supposes that everything exists in a **state**, and that this state can be quantified in mechanistic terms, such as temperature, ambient pressure, velocity, coefficient of expansion, specific gravity, and others. The interplay between states and dynamic laws is such that, given the law, the state of a system determines its state at all subsequent moments. This element of determinism that Newton built into mechanics has grown to pervade all science. It forms the basis of scientific testing by providing for the possibility of prediction.

The procedure of breaking down physical systems into their elementary components and looking for an explanation of their behavior at the lowest level is called **reductionism,** and it has exercised a powerful influence over scientific thinking. There even exists a philosophy known as Lagrangian, named after the French physicist, Joseph Lagrange, where once a well-defined mathematical procedure accurately describes the system, then the behavior of the system is explained. In short, a Lagrangian equals an explanation. Many physicists believe that the entire universe will one day be explained by a Lagrangian.

Darwin's theory of evolution, along with genetics and molecular biology, led biologists to a strongly mechanistic and reductionistic approach to the study of biological sciences. Living organisms are today generally regarded as purely complex machines at the molecular level. This scientific paradigm has led to many important advances and discoveries, and no doubt contributed to our greater understanding of living things. Analysis and reduction will always have a central role to play in science, but they are limited in explaining a great portion of the phenomena of life. **In other words, the whole does not equal the sum of the parts.** One cannot imagine dissecting every molecule of a monarch butterfly and discovering how this lovely creature migrates thousands of miles to the same place it was born. We still have no idea how a salmon finds the river of its birth and swims up stream to spawn and die. There are so many things that are greater than the sum of the parts, and that is why the study of physics has evolved and may surpass the biologists in explaining the essence of life.

Most researchers are obsessed with numbers. The nineteenth century physicist, Lord Kelvin, used similar logic when he said, "When you can measure what you are speaking about and express it in numbers, you know something about it. But when you cannot - your knowledge is of a meagre and unsatisfactory kind." But as famed writer and cancer researcher, Lewis Thomas, wrote, "Kelvin may have had things exactly the wrong way around. The task of converting observations into numbers is the last task rather than the first task to be done, and can only be done when you have learned, beforehand, a great deal about the observations themselves. You can, to be sure, achieve a very deep understanding of nature by quantitative measurements, but you must know what you are talking about before you can apply the numbers to predictions." In Kelvin's case, his obsession led to a colossal blunder. Using what was then known about the sources of energy and the loss of energy from the physics of that day, he calculated that neither the earth nor the sun were older than a few million years. This caused a considerable stir among biological and geographical circles, especially the evolutionists. Darwin himself challenged these numbers as the period of time was much too short for his theory of evolution. Kelvin was soon proven wrong and his mistake completely ruined his credibility.

Lewis Thomas says health researchers are dealing with an inexact science and "this hankering to turn their disciplines into exact sciences is physics envy." What is even more startling is that the health researchers have neglected to keep pace with their fellow physicists. As Paul Davies, in his book, **THE COSMIC BLUEPRINT**, states ,"It is often said that physicists invented the mechanistic-reductionist philosophy, taught it to the biologists, and then abandoned it themselves. It cannot be denied that modern physics has a strongly holistic, even teleological flavour, and that this is due in large part to the influence of the quantum theory."

I ask that my fellow dental researchers consider

the substance growing below the gumline producing an inflammatory response and ultimately destroying the supporting structures of the teeth to be an ecosystem. It is certainly complex enough and seems quite capable of adapting to changes. The actions of the spirochetes suggest that there is a sense of **global cooperation** among the various bacteria and **self-organization**, not to mention **unpredictable behavior** and **uniqueness**. One only needs to observe the bacterial mat for a short time to gain a real sense of **vitalism**. And anyone who has monitored the bacteria during treatment knows they possess a very strong **will to survive**. Given this level of complexity, it seems logical to assume that the mat possesses an ability to adapt to slight changes in environment.

If anyone were given the task of destroying a larger macroscopic ecosystem, say a coral reef (which is surprisingly similar), it would not seem prudent to harvest all the creatures living on the reef and attempt to determine the specific role each plays. It would make better sense to study the **relationships** of the organisms, perhaps discovering food chains, etc. , so the removal of certain vital parts could destroy the entire ecosystem. Physicists are certainly leaning toward such holistic thinking. What Paul Keyes was saying is that the large motile organisms seem to be important to the vitality of the entire ecosystem, maybe as protectors from the body's defenses. At the very least, using phase contrast microscopy is a quick and inexpensive way of observing if bacteria are still alive. It serves as a quality control system, similar to monitoring the bacterium, E. coli, to assure the safety of swimming pools. The E. coli are harmless, but it is rationalized that if this organism thrives, other harmful bacteria could be thriving too, and the pool is therefore unsafe. Couldn't we say that persons with disease associated motile bacteria are at risk and we should eliminate this risk to assure the periodontal health of our patients? Given the epidemic incidence of this disease, we certainly need some type of monitoring and our treatment rationale should not fare any worse than current modalities.

There is no doubt that eliminating the subgingival motile organisms has eliminated the bacterial mat itself in over ninety per cent of treated cases. Far too many clinicians are reporting this level of success. Such high percentages of success are considered marvelous in treating other disease entities and are far and away better than any other mode of treatment offered in dentistry.

Once again, I find solace in Lewis Thomas as he says, "Science, especially twentieth century science, has provided us with a glimpse of something we never really knew before, the revelation of human ignorance. We have been used to the belief, down one century after another, that we more or less comprehend everything bar one or two mysteries like the mental processes of our gods. Every age, not just the eighteenth century, has regarded itself as the Age of Reason, and we have never lacked for explanations of the world and its ways. Now all is being brought up short, and this has been the work of science. We have a wilderness of mystery to make our way through in the centuries ahead, and we will need science, but not science alone. Science will produce the data and some meaning in the data, but never the full meaning. For getting the full grasp, for perceiving real significance when significance is at hand, we shall need minds from all sorts of brains outside the fields of science, most of all the brains of poets, of course, but also those of artists, musicians, philosophers, historians, writers in general."

May I add that health researchers need to listen to the clinicians out in the trenches dealing with all the complexities involved in successful treatment.

There is a positive note that will be discussed in detail later, and that is there are several antiseptic agents currently in the research stage that should change the tide rather quickly. These antiseptics are dissolved in time-released biodegradable polymers. This means professionals will be able to inject the material below the gumline, where the material hardens and slowly dissolves causing a constant dilute amount of antiseptic to be released over a long period of time - possibly weeks. Such materials will quickly change the course of dental treatment.

# Chapter 4
# THE ESSENCE OF LIFE

There is one unfinished item before leaving the bacterial mat. Our discussion of *organization* offers some insights into life itself and warrants a short deviation from dental disease. Quantum mechanics has brought about explosions of new thinking and theoretical physicists are still digesting the data. There are, however, several other significant discoveries and the beginning of life is starting to unfold.

Everyone agrees that all nature is filled with boundless order. But all things have not yet been created. We see evidence that the world is creating and changing in totally unpredictable ways. No one could ever have predicted that when electrons were sufficiently excited, trillions of them would suddenly cooperate in a rhythmic pattern to create the laser. Quantum mechanics itself is baffling as there does not seem to be particulate mass to electrons. If one could stack them one on top of the other, no one knows if they would take up space, and if they did, how much. Quantum mechanics then, is based on statistical analysis rather than actual measurement. Therefore, a new set of laws needs to be developed that may differ greatly from Newtonian laws. It is hoped that these new laws will shed light on living structures to exhibit, through organized electron activity, global cooperation, or the ability of living matter to exert influence on other living matter that is distant and seemingly not connected.

I believe that we are going to find that a force as pervasive as gravity will be discovered explaining self organization. No doubt there are at least two laws, one governing inorganic matter which explains the continuity of the universe and molecular cohesion, and a similar but more powerful force that forms carbon, oxygen, nitrogen, hydrogen and sulfur into the complex molecular structures that become proteins and, eventually, living cells.

There is evidence that the earth itself functions as an individual organism. Over the last several million years the intensity of the sun has increased about thirty per cent, yet through atmospheric manipulations the earth has managed to keep a relatively constant temperature (except for minor aberrations like the glacial age) to sustain the evolving life forms.

We have some insights into the complex nature of life. This was stumbled upon by Mandelbrot, who discovered that when mathematical formulas plotted on an X and Y axis reach a certain complex state they form unpredictable and bizarre patterns that are in themselves complex and repetitive. This startling finding was called a *fractal* and hints that complex global patterns in nature may be the result of such fractals. Other experiments in the realm of Chaos show there may be no such thing, as most things that appear chaotic and random can be explained through relatively simple deterministic algorithms. Experiments have produced patterns that are similar to coastlines and migratory routes of birds.

Von Neumann's book, **THEORY OF SELF-REPRODUCING AUTOMATA**, found that self-reproduction can only occur when the machine exceeds a certain threshold of complexity. This means that complexity is responsible for forms taking on new and different qualities. A related phenomenon is "video feedback" where a television camera is focused on its monitor and after adjustments, gives off bizarre complex patterns.

It seems, through all this, that several new principles are developing. The principle of complexity being the first. This is followed by self organization. In my way of thinking, self organization would best be described as the AFFINITY TO ORGANIZE. This principle probably has variable strengths depending on the make-up and arrangement of DNA proteins. This would explain why so many different creatures formed at different levels of complexity. I am not sure why we are the only creatures to evolve to the highest level of complexity.

Quantum physics may show how electrons are used by proteins to influence distant proteins in the principle of global cooperation. Although it seems most plausible that such cooperation could be explained in the affinity to organize principle, there are other considerations, such as vitalism or self preservation, which seem to drive organization. One final characteristic of life forms is uniqueness. Even individual bacteria are unique from one another and their offspring have their own unique characteristics. This is as yet a complete mystery and will be left to future generations. Discovering the mechanisms of the AFFINITY TO ORGANIZE principle is enough to keep the most intelligent minds busy for some time. We need to return to the simpler problems of dealing with dental infections. Since we have discussed the bacteria existing below the gumline, let us now look at decay problems above the gumline.

# Chapter 5
# DENTAL CARIES AS A MICROBIAL INFECTION

Above the gumline an entirely different picture exists. The body has developed a remarkable system to protect itself against bacterial invasion. The most important part of this system is saliva. It is hard to think of spit as wonderful, but this sticky fluid performs an extremely complex function.

First, the mucin provides a continuous membranous coating around the teeth and soft tissues, like a snug-fitting glove. This is important because the outer layers of tooth structure consist of a porous enamel that can easily demineralize and become chalky. The protein coat not only holds moisture, but actually helps remineralize areas affected by acids or dryness. It will hinder bacteria from attaching to tooth structure which is something bacteria must do to cause decay. It also aids in trapping chemicals from foods that give us our sense of taste, making it a vital part of our daily enjoyment of eating.

There are proteins providing other important functions. Enzymes such as Amylase, start the digestive process by breaking down starches to smaller molecules. When a cracker or a slice of bread is eaten, this enzyme goes immediately to work and, as everyone knows, the bread or cracker is almost dissolved very quickly. Other enzymes, such as Lactoperoxidase and Lysozyme, digest bacteria and provide a first line attack on mouth-loving bacteria. Certain bacteria produce peroxides to neutralize the enzymes which release oxygen. This is one reason why saliva tends to foam. Another reason is that there are detergents and buffering components that discourage bacterial colony formation. Add large amounts of antibodies and sodium bicarbonate, and saliva appears most formidable against bacteria.

How, then, did decay become an epidemic problem? Actually, it was not much of a problem until around the sixteenth century when sugars were first refined and tea and crumpets became the afternoon rage. People did not follow any form of dental hygiene in those days and the bacteria were left to do whatever they pleased. Certain bacteria changed in the presence of sugars and became much more aggressive. They actually grew minute filaments out of their cell walls. This allowed them to stick together and break through the protein barrier and adhere to tooth enamel. Their acids and other waste products leached the calcium out of the enamel, softening it and allowing other bacteria to soak in and slowly eat away the tooth structure. No doubt, decay affected almost everyone up until recent times, but what is the incidence today?

First we must look at who is prone to decay. A comprehensive four year study of 30,000 children, ages five to fourteen, living in ten communities provides interesting data. This study was funded by the Robert Wood Johnson Foundation and five of the communi-

ties had fluoridated water and five did not. It was designed to assess whether caries could be reduced or eliminated by professional applications of fluorides and sealants, regular use of fluoride rinses and classroom education. The most significant findings were:
- Program participants had dramatically less decay than had been expected.
- A substantial number of children had no cavities at all.
- Fluoride mouthrinses were far less effective than previously reported.
- The overwhelming importance of water fluoridation.
- Cost of delivering comprehensive preventive care was far more expensive than previous estimates.
- Some twenty per cent of the children accounted for sixty per cent of all decay found.

The last finding is most significant as it points out the need to identify those individuals who are at risk of decay and concentrate expensive ($52 per child per year) preventive procedures on the "at risk" patients. Today, prevention is performed blindly on every patient with no thought as to whether it is needed or not.

So how do we identify these individuals? We do know they seem to have lower levels of zinc, iron, and copper in their saliva. Also caries resistant saliva appears to have better buffering capacity. The amount of salivary flow is definitely a factor as is the amount and the frequency of ingested sugars. The position and surface roughness of the teeth are important. But these factors are fairly difficult to assess and can only be done with careful professional observation and expensive laboratory tests.

There is a simpler way. The main bacteria causing decay is Streptococcus mutans. This organism, no matter which of the above causes exists, will rise as the risk of caries rises. We can use a rather inexpensive test for Strep. mutans and identify those individuals who are prone to decay and treat them before decay starts.

Such a test actually exists today and all parents should ask their dentist to perform the test. The method of treatment for children should be modified as follows:

The current "prophy" or cleaning should not be blindly given. Most children do not need to have their teeth polished by an abrasive paste and there is evidence that such polishing is more harmful than helpful. If there is obvious stain or tartar, then the child could be scheduled for cleaning. What should be done on a routine exam is to detect any sign of disease and take a sample of the saliva for a Strep. mutans test. Results of the test are read after a forty-eight hour incubation period and those patients who are "at risk" are contacted for further treatment. This eliminates blind fluoride treatments, sealants, etc. , for the majority who are not "at risk." Obviously, if active disease is found, the patient is "at risk" and should be treated accordingly. Subsequent visits would then include the laboratory tests to see if the risk has been lowered or eliminated.

The goal of treatment should be to eliminate the

bacteria causing dental caries and if the Strep. mutans test, or similar test is used, we can soon eliminate decay once and for all.

If treatment is necessary, it would include dietary counseling and custom trays that are worn ten minutes a day with a prescription grade fluoride gel in the tray. The patient is asked to chew on the trays to squish the fluoride in and around the surfaces of the teeth. We can gain a surprise benefit from such treatment, as not only will decay be arrested, but certain affected areas will *remineralize*. This means that teeth plagued with cavities may not need to be restored by a dentist with silver or plastic filling materials.

This is a tremendously important factor as there are an estimated **one billion** cavities currently existing in the United States population. Over fifteen per cent of the entire amount of health care dollars spent each year involves dental treatment, and caries is still the single most expensive part of that cost.

Dental caries is still a serious health problem which touches many members of society with cost, pain and discomfort. We have made great strides in reducing its incidence with the advent of fluoride, but the most significant gains have not involved the dentist, but rather the water treatment authority. The dentist still sees decay as a cleaning and dietary problem, which only involves him in restoring the damage. By demanding a caries risk test and treatment for eliminating the bacteria causing caries, we could eliminate decay rather quickly.

The majority of the television advertisements on dental products are somewhat misleading as claims are made about how fantastic they are. About ninety-nine percent of a toothpaste consists of fillers, abrasives and good tasting elements. The ads are based on the abrasives' ability to clean the teeth. There is good reason to keep the ads in this arena because mechanical cleaning comes under "cosmetic" claims and, therefore, is not subject to FDA (Federal Drug Administration) approval. The only item worthwhile is the fluoride, although there is some confusion about effective concentrations. What I find most appalling is that many of the leading toothpastes use sorbitol as a sweetener and sorbitol will grow Strep. mutans. So a person may be lulled into a false sense of security by brushing fastidiously, only to grow large numbers of bacteria that can cause decay. Then, if there is exposure to sugar and the bacteria have a heyday growing large populations and overwhelming the mouth's natural defenses, a cavity might begin.

There are simple agents that have the potential of preventing decay. Bicarbonate of soda is one of the least expensive ways to prevent both decay and gum disease. There is a new toothpaste with both soda and fluoride that should have a major impact on dental diseases and it is highly recommended.

Several companies have stretched their claims to the point where the FDA is taking them to task. Mostly they are in the area of mouthrinses which have inconsistent research data. I personally do not routinely recommend mouthrinses except for Viadent. Their research has been fairly comprehensive and if it is used exactly as they recommend it seems to be beneficial.

A prescription mouthrinse, Peridex, has chlorhexidine as its active ingredient. This has been shown to be one of the best available antimicrobial agents, although it is expensive and I tend to find other, less expensive, agents for treatment. No doubt, it does have some value in fighting decay and gingivitis.

It is interesting to note that Europe has far more brands of dentifrices on the market with antimicrobial potential. It may be that our toothpaste manufacturers have waged such a competitive struggle that they tend to avoid adding agents that might cause the FDA to require expensive research to substantiate claims. Fortunately, that obstacle will soon change as the enlightened public will demand better products.

To round out our perspective, it seems most fitting that we examine the profession charged with the responsibility for maintaining our dental health— look at its history, how it perceived dental problems in the past, and how modern practices are currently dealing with the problems.

# Chapter 6
# THE HISTORY OF DENTISTRY

A look into the past will help you better understand the evolution of the modern dentist and why we think the way we do. There have been people interested in dentistry since recorded history. This is natural since dental diseases have inflicted so much suffering. It is only logical that there have always been those individuals trying to relieve their comrade's pain.

Physicians have always expressed interest in dental pain, but they were hard pressed by more life threatening conditions, although many of the original dental writings were by physicians. In the United States the need caused barbers and blacksmiths to become involved. They developed crude tools for removing teeth (one was called an odontodogon) and dentures were fabricated from iron, ivory, and wood. Of course, advanced gum disease made the teeth easier to extract and a couple large nips of whiskey made the extraction bearable. George Washington was in constant pain from his teeth through most of his early adult life. Eventually, he had them extracted and the ensuing ill-fitting dentures (some are on display at the American History Museum of The Smithsonian Institute and the University of Maryland Dental School) were the reason he never smiled in his portraits.

Since the demand was great, a few individuals

traveled to Europe where a fledgling dental profession existed and offered apprentice training. Returning home they became the original American Dentists and they were so successful, that in 1839 the Baltimore College of Dental Surgery became the first dental college in the world. Five students comprised the class. Only two finished to earn a degree—D.D.S., Doctor of Dental Surgery (*surgery* since extractions were the most prominent part of the dental practice).

In the late 1800's classic stories about dentists have been told. People like "Painless Parker," who traveled the West setting up shop on street corners, amazed people with the ability to remove a tooth with the speed of a magician's hands, and often without very much pain.

## Anesthesia

The history of anesthesia and its development through the dental profession is one of the most interesting stories of all. There is evidence that even in ancient times surgical procedures were a valuable means of treatment. The problem was that often pain from surgery was more severe than the disorder itself.

We know that surgical pain can be controlled by rendering a patient unconscious. Even in the Bible, we find that "God caused a deep sleep to fall over Adam. And while Adam slept, God removed one of his ribs and closed up the flesh."

Early man himself discovered anesthetics to control pain. Ancient Indians described sammohine, the fumes of a burning hashish hemp—marijuana, the inhalation of which permitted medical and dental operations. Other types of medication were derived from the juices of opium, mandrake, and certain hemlocks.

The effects of ether have been known for some time. An Arabian chemist named Yarbear wrote about it as early as the twelfth century. But for many, many years it was considered just a curiosity that would cause exhilarating effects when inhaled. In 1842 Crawford W. Long from Jefferson, Georgia, discovered ether also had anesthetic value. He successfully performed several minor surgical procedures using ether, but did little to publicize his work, probably not realizing its potential value.

Because of the absence of potent anesthetics, major surgery was rarely possible. Surgical techniques were held back and limited to only certain small procedures, basically corrective and patch amputations and the sewing of large tears in the skin. It was actually back in 1773 that nitrous oxide was initially discovered by Priestly. Nitrous oxide was later called "laughing gas" because it elevated the person's mood and laughter usually resulted. Inhalation of nitrous oxide caused many to "giggle, dance, and act in a zany fashion, often enjoying very wild ideas."

On a fateful day , December 10, 1844, in Hartford, Connecticut, a public demonstration on the uses of nitrous oxide was advertised. The gas was to be administered to all who wished to inhale it, after paying the 25 cents admission. Dr. Horace Wells, a

Hartford dentist, attended the presentation with a friend named Cooley. When volunteers were called, Mr. Cooley inhaled the gas, but instead of laughing and dancing around like most, he began fighting. While struggling, his foot caught behind a bench and he fell heavily, forcing his leg over a sharp object. As Cooley rose, Wells noticed a wide, bleeding gash, yet Cooley seemed oblivious to pain. Wells, alerted to the significance of the event, discussed it with a dental colleague, Dr. Riggs. Determined to try the gas himself, Dr. Wells bought a leather bagful of the gas from the lecturer and seated in his own office, inhaled the gas to insensibility. On December 11, 1844, Dr. Riggs painlessly pulled one of Wells' molars and the grand discovery of gas anesthesia was born to the world.

Dr. Wells proceeded to successfully use nitrous oxide in his practice. His enthusiasm grew and wishing to share his discovery with the world, he traveled to Boston to visit a prominent dentist, Dr. William T. Morton. As Morton listened, he became very interested and contacted a physician friend, Dr. S. C. Warren, convincing him to set up a demonstration at Massachusetts General Hospital.

Dr. Wells was a very timid, insecure person and on the day of the demonstration, he gasped as he walked into the surgical suite where a large audience of students and physicians had gathered. All were extremely skeptical that a lowly dentist had anything to contribute to the medical profession and they laughed impolitely. Dr. Warren did not help matters by sarcastically introducing Wells, inciting jeers and laughter from the group. Dr. Warren ordered Wells to proceed.

Nervously, Dr. Wells put a leather bag over the patient's mouth and nose. It is unclear whether the nitrous oxide Wells used was pure or had been contaminated by air. The outcome was that the patient moaned and rolled around on the table. Wells began to perspire nervously as his audience became more unruly, loudly laughing and jeering. After a time, the patient seemed to calm down somewhat and Wells instructed the physicians to begin. As the knife entered the skin, the patient let out a bloodcurdling scream and Dr. Wells left in shame. Deeply scarred by this ridicule, he returned to Hartford where his melancholy forced him to close his office for several months.

Meanwhile, his old friend, Dr. Morton in Boston, remained curious about the use of nitrous oxide. He consulted a physician proficient in chemistry named Dr. Jackson, who suggested that he might also wish to try ether, since it could more readily be produced. Dr. Morton devised a system of dripping ether on a cloth and having the patient breathe the vapors. On his first attempt, he successfully extracted a tooth without pain.

Being an enterprising person, Dr. Morton saw the benefits of this discovery and consulted an attorney. Receiving a release from Dr. Jackson, he immediately applied for a patent for inhalation anesthesia. Once again, he approached Dr. Warren at Massachusetts General Hospital for another demonstration. Because Dr. Morton was more self assured and overcame the impoliteness of his audience, he calmed his patient by telling him to breathe deeply. The surgeon removed a tumor from the unconscious patient's neck without

any noticeable pain. The news of Dr. Morton's
achievement spread very fast and when Dr. Wells read
about his fame, he took his own life.

Many people in the medical and dental professions
knew, however, of Dr. Wells and they insisted that the
American Dental and Medical Associations investi-
gate. In 1864 the ADA publicly declared that Horace
Wells was the discoverer of inhalation anesthesia and
in 1870 the AMA followed suit. As we know, ether went
on to become the major general anesthetic for many
years. However, it was impractical to use in dentistry
as it required a mask over the patient's face during the
entire procedure. Thus nitrous oxide seemed a better
anesthesia for dentistry.

Unfortunately, nitrous oxide is a fairly weak anesthetic with several disadvantages. A person becomes
sedate in the early stages, but just before unconsciousness, an excitatory period occurs that makes many
people hard to control, which probably explains what
happened to Cooley and Dr. Wells' patient. The anesthetic is not strong enough to carry the patient through
this period and into true anesthesia unless the percentage of oxygen is dropped below the level necessary to
sustain human life (20%).

Observing this, a man named McKesson devised a
method where a person could be taken through the
excitatory phase and down to unconsciousness. He
accomplished this by reducing the level of oxygen to
10%, leaving 90% nitrous oxide. The person was taken
down into unconsciousness, while the administrator
carefully watched the lips. When the lips and finger-
nails turned blue, the oxygen was quickly turned up to

keep the patient from being asphyxiated. This type of anesthetic was given for years, and many a grandparent can tell tales about the dental chairs with big straps to hold you down so you would not injure yourself while going through the excitatory phase or struggling against being asphyxiated.

As you may have guessed, many people died from this type of anesthesia so the use of nitrous oxide was phased out in the 1950's. Yet it was revived again in the late 1960's, but this time it was not used to put people to sleep, only to induce a level of anesthesia where the patient experienced a mood elevation, a sense of relaxation and well-being, and the capacity to withstand mild pain without local anesthetic.

Recently, its use has been challenged by studies that show pregnant women to be far more susceptible to spontaneous abortion if chronically exposed to even very low levels of nitrous oxide.

## Local Anesthetics

The use of hollow needles piercing the flesh has been used for centuries naturally—stings from insects, bites by poisonous snakes—to inject a paralyzing poison into the flesh of its victim. By this manner, such creatures are able to immobilize their prey and eat them at will. In 1844, the first hypodermic needle was invented by Dr. Ryne in Edinburgh, Scotland. He probably never dreamed what would happen to his invention and all the uses and ramifications of it. His needles were quite large and the syringes crude and primarily devised for the use of morphine to reduce very severe pain.

In 1846, Dr. Albert Neiman, a dentist working in Vienna was studying the anesthetic, cocaine. Derived from the cocoa weed, cocaine was discovered in South America being chewed by the Indians—similar to chewing tobacco. Chewing of this cocoa weed would anesthetize the stomach lining, lessening hunger, and providing a stimulating effect to the person chewing it. Dr. Neiman isolated cocaine from the cocoa weed and, later that year, Carl Koeler, a medical colleague, discovered that cocaine painted in the mouth acted as a topical anesthetic to stop gagging while examining the throat. Dilute solutions of the narcotic also aided in giving eye examinations.

It is quite possible that the first injection of a local anesthetic occurred in 1865 during the United States Civil War. If a soldier received a facial wound, a face mask for general anesthesia could not be used, but a surgeon found injecting morphine locally allowed him to operate while the patient was still awake.

In Baltimore in 1885, Dr. William Hulsted used cocaine injections to block the nerves of the jaw, permitting painless dental surgery. The National Dental Association awarded him a medal for his discovery. Soon many dentists possessed powdered cocaine which was mixed with boiling water to be used in an anesthetic syringe.

During World War I, Dr. Harvey Cook was annoyed with the fact that cocaine had to be mixed in fresh batches for every use. He thought of sealing the solutions against contamination by mixing batches into individual cartridges which could be injected by an intersealing rubber stopper moving through as a plunger. He tried clean, brass Army cartridges, cut lengths of glass tubing, and sealed the ends with rubber pencil erasures. His technique became popular, but as cocaine for dental injections increased, the side-effects were more noticeable. It irritated tissue and sometimes would cause large areas to slough off at the injection site.

Alternatives to cocaine were being researched by many people, including Alfred Einhardt in 1900, as he tried to separate cocaine's anesthetic abilities from the irritating qualities. In 1905 Braun introduced novocaine (Novo meaning new) and novocaine eliminated cocaine's toxicity. The drug was further refined and synthesized now using the name Procaine. In use for many years, this drug became the standard dental anesthetic.

In the 1960's other local anesthetics were developed from completely different molecular structures— the most popular being Xylocaine which became the parent of a new family of injectables. The mechanism for sealing cartridges, now called carpules, had been perfected and was available in sterile packages so each patient received a new sterile, disposable carpule for every injection. Also in the 1960's, disposable needles were developed that were always sharp and greatly lessened the pain from injections.

### Denture Era

Armed with these new anesthetics, dentists became more and more skilled at removing teeth. As the number of extractions increased so did the interest in replacing them with some type of denture. At the same time Wells discovered nitrous oxide, Charles Goodyear was working with a new material from the juices of certain tropical rubber plants and he discovered how to stabilize and harden these juices. Giving it the name of vulcanite, he obtained a patent in 1851. At first, rubber was primarily used for thin layers or coatings such as the MacIntosh raincoat developed in Scotland. The uses for rubber grew at an unbelievable rate and fortunes were made as new ideas materialized. When it became possible to mold and harden rubber, it was like a miracle to dentistry. Impressions of jaws were taken with Plaster of Paris and stone models made. The rubber was then molded onto the model creating a base for teeth far more accurately and simply than anything imaginable. Affordable dentures were quickly produced by the mechanically adept dentists and the profession exploded with growth.

An interesting sidelight of the story was that during this period in American history, control of new industries could be easily gained through patents. In 1868 a businessman named Joshua Bacon gained control of the vulcanizing process. Bacon demanded fees from individual dentists starting from $25 to $100 a year, depending on the size of the practice, plus $1 for each denture replacing up to five teeth and $2 for dentures with six or more teeth. Bacon had spies traveling throughout the country examining the patient records of dentists. These were tough and intimidating men and Bacon advertised in newspapers threatening to prosecute any dentist violating his patent rights. As you might expect, dentists resented this attitude and despite the value of vulcanized dentures, many refused to make them. Bacon was a hated man and on April 13, 1879, was found shot to death in a San Francisco hotel. At first, the police were baffled as there was no robbery and a motive could not be found, but their investigation uncovered the resentment of dentists and soon Dr. Samuel Chafont surrendered to police. Chafont, a dentist from Wilmington, Delaware, had been prevented by a court order from using vulcanite. When Chafont moved to San Francisco, Bacon followed and resumed legal proceedings and threatened him with prison. Chafont had gone to Bacon's hotel room to frighten him, but his gun fired accidently and he was sentenced to ten years in San Quentin for manslaughter. In 1881, the patent rights expired and the use of vulcanite flourished.

## Fillings

The earliest fillings were soft materials that did not strengthen the tooth, but only filled the cavities, providing relief by insulating the tooth from air and saliva. Probably the first metal filling was a pure, soft gold leaf or foil. Such gold foil carefully placed in the cavity bit by bit with great pressure would wedge the pieces together until they were welded into a singular mass. Such restorations are superb fillings, but the process takes special skill, often taking hours for one filling. As you would guess, such a procedure is extremely expensive, available to only a few, and the difficulty in placing was further enhanced because any contamination by saliva whatsoever would cause failure of the restoration. It is interesting to note that such a filling is still the standard test used by State Board examinations for dental licensing, even though only one in over a million fillings placed today are gold foil and 90% of the dentists in this country do not use them at all.

Mercury is a constituent of many dental fillings. It is a fascinating metal, being the only metal liquid at room temperatures. It hardens and freezes solid like other metals at thirty seven degrees below fahrenheit. Silver in color, it is impossible to pick up as it easily slips between the fingers. For a long time, mercury was called "quick silver." Any alloy of metal containing silver is called an amalgam and the most commonly used dental filling is the silver amalgam.

The first use of silver amalgam was described by M. Taveau, a Parisian dentist, in 1832. He filed *powdered silver from coins,* mixed with mercury and made a soft putty-like mass that he called "silver paste." He placed it into a tooth cavity and it hardened or amalgamated as the silver powder and mercury dissolved into each other. It was inexpensive and worked well, but had some disadvantages. The filling often expanded inside the tooth, splitting it apart or raised above the tooth, causing improper biting and pain. The swelling process varied depending on the purity of the coins and the amount of contamination from saliva, since many aspects of the process were not understood. It was not until later that the addition of copper greatly enhanced the material and the addition of zinc would scavenge the moisture so the dimensions remained stable.

To a large extent, the success of silver fillings depends on the skill of the dentist to properly prepare the tooth so the filling and tooth are stronger as a completed unit. Today the intimate nature of dental materials and tooth preparation are well known, but early on, the lack of skill and contamination of the amalgam brought varied results which caused confusion as the use of these fillings spread throughout the world.

An interesting story occurred in the 1830's when two Frenchmen, the Crawcour brothers, came to New York City. With a fanfare of publicity, they introduced a remarkable filling material, scientifically developed in Europe, called royal mineral succedaneum. These two charming and witty brothers demonstrated their product with zeal and showed many filling examples in extracted teeth and their own mouths. The American dentists, hungry for a better restoration, bought enormous amounts of succedaneum. But it was a rather poor grade of silver amalgam and, in a short period, it became apparent that the new substance was not very good. The Crawcour brothers gained substantial wealth but left considerable damage and caused such a great struggle within the dental profession that it was called "The Great Amalgam War." Many of the profession's most prominent dentists were violently against the use of silver fillings and spread the word that silver fillings were poisonous and detrimental to health. They called upon their medical colleagues and

many found many agreeable ears. A completely new
society called the American Society of Dental Surgeons was formed in 1840 and declared that the use of
amalgam was malpractice. The Society demanded
that members sign a pledge—"I pledge that I will
never, under any circumstances, use it in my practice
as a dental surgeon." So the "Amalgam War" raged on
and many dentists were ostracized for using silver
fillings as the Society spread the word that these
dentists were not to be trusted. (This is not too
different from the reaction we received early on after
introducing the Keyes technique, but like "amalgam,"
we knew we were right).

During all this, a few dentists were continuing to
experiment independently. Thomas Evans in Paris in
1848 mixed tin with silver and mercury and, instead of
expanding, it shrank. Cadmium seemed to reduce the
shrinkage. When he reported this, many experimen-
ters, their curiosity raised, tested many metal addi-
tives. As time went on, the proper ratio of tin, silver,
mercury, copper and other metals was perfected to the
point where there was neither shrinkage nor expansion.

An American dentist by the name of G.B. Black
was probably the most prominent American researcher in silver amalgam. Dr. Black invented a machine
that would measure the amount of biting or chewing
force exerted by the jaws, revealing that over 325
pounds per square inch could be exerted by hard
chewing. He also noted the necessity of the metals to
be pure. He developed a new, highly acceptable metal
formula that is still the standard of today. Dr. Black

developed new tooth-cutting instruments and is most remembered for his design of tooth cavity preparations, and his famous phrase "extension for prevention" guided dentists to prepare teeth so the filling would extend into all areas prone to decay. His principles are still the basis for cavity design taught in most dental schools today.

Radiographs or x-rays were brought to the dental practice in the 1930's enhancing the now sophisticated dental practitioner. The 1940's brought on affluence and people began to spend more and more money on repairing their teeth and the profession responded by creating experts or specialists in many of the dental disciplines. Now there were oral surgeons to do the difficult extractions and perform surgery on the jaws, pedodontists to concentrate on specific problems of children, orthodontists to straighten teeth, endodontists to do the more difficult root canal fillings, prosthodontists to do complex reconstruction where there are several missing teeth, and periodontists to deal with gum diseases.

Today the swing is in the opposite direction with general dentists doing more and more complex procedures. The fastest growing post-graduate course is the "comprehensive general dental residency", which involves one to two years in a residency training program after graduating from dental school. These programs teach aspiring residents to perform most known procedures in dentistry. This has the potential to provide more efficient and, hopefully, less costly care (one stop shopping) for dental patients in the future.

# Chapter 7
# THE HISTORY OF
# ORAL MICROBIOLOGY

We know from paleopathological studies that man has been subject to periodontal diseases since prehistoric times. In earlier times, these diseases were a major problem and evidence from human skeletal remains show they were rampant—far worse than the incidence of decay. In the embalmed bodies of Egyptians 4,000 years old it is quite evident. Earliest recordings reveal that worms were thought to cause tooth decay and all kinds of methods were devised to drive them out. Latin writings speak of "fumigations" and others used the seeds of henbane, leeks, and onions to drive out the worms. The Chinese believed the worm theory as late as the beginning of this century. Their term for tooth decay or hollow tooth is "chung choo," which is similar to the Japanese term, "mushi ba" —mushi = worm, ba = tooth. Attempts to treat periodontal disease were recorded in ancient writings revealing oral hygiene practices by the Sumaritans of 3,000 B.C. and elaborately decorated golden toothpicks were found in excavations in Mesopotamia suggesting an interest in cleanliness of the mouth. Sumaritans describe a gingival massage combined with various herbal medications as a treatment for gum disease.

Mouthwashes were also employed and there are references to six different drugs suggesting treatment of sickness of the mouth.

In Chinese medical writings around 2500 B.C. oral disease is divided into three types: 1) Fong Ya or inflammatory conditions; 2) Ya Kon or disease of the soft investive tissues around the teeth; 3) Chong Ya or dental caries. The gingival conditions are described in great detail and herbal remedies were mentioned for their treatment. The Chinese were among the earliest people to use a juice stick as a toothpick or toothbrush to clean the mouth and to massage the gingival tissue.

Early Hebrews recognized the importance of oral hygiene through observations of oral and pathological conditions of the teeth. The surrounding tissues were described in Talmudic writings. The Phoenician civilization included a specimen of wire splinting apparently constructed to stabilize teeth loosened by chronic gum disease. Among the ancient Greeks, Hippocrates, the Father of modern medicine, was the first to institute a careful examination of the patient's pulse, temperature, respiration, sputum, pains, and excreta. He discussed the function of the eruption of teeth and also the cause of gum diseases. He believed that the inflammation of the gums could be produced by the accumulation of calculus with gum bleeding occurring in cases of persistent disease. Descriptions of different varieties of splenic maladies were assigned the following symptoms: "the belly is swollen, the spleen is large and hard, the patient suffers from acute pain, the gums are detached from the teeth and smell bad."

The Etruscans in 700 B.C. were adept in the art of constructing artificial dentures, but there is no evidence that they were aware as to why teeth were lost. The Romans referred to gum diseases and advised, "if the gums separate from the teeth it is beneficial to chew unripe pears and apples and keep the juices in the mouth." They described looseness of the teeth caused by weakness of the roots and flaccidity of the gums. It was noted for these cases the necessity to touch the gums lightly with a red-hot iron and then smear them with honey.

It is evident that the Romans used toothbrushes as it is mentioned in the writings of many Roman poets. Gum massage was an integral part of their oral hygiene. Paul of Aegina, during the seventh century, described abscesses of the gum and wrote that tartar build-up must be removed either with scrapers or small files and the teeth should be carefully cleaned after the last meal of the day. This recognition of tartar as the causative agent was mentioned by Rhazes (850—923), an Arabian, who was a voluminous writer and who had seven chapters on the care of teeth. Also a set of instruments designed by Albucasis for the use of scaling has been noted. In the fifteenth century, Valescus of Montpelier (1382—1417) said that in order to treat diseases of the gums tartar must be removed little by little. References were also made to the use of white wine, roasted salt and aromatic substances as adjuncts to periodontal therapy.

As the fledgling profession of dental surgeon became more crystallized, it became natural for these surgeons to concentrate on the removal of tartar which became synonymous with periodontal treatment. In keeping with the rest of dental therapy, such mechanical procedures were quite easy to implement. They ignored the work of Von Leeuwenhoek, who in 1685 noted moving "animolecules" (live bacteria) while taking samples from his teeth and observing them through his new invention, the microscope. No doubt, Leeuwenhoek had remembered earlier writings that made reference to some type of antimicrobial therapy when he placed a drop of wine vinegar on the "animolecules" and they "fell dead forthwith." But early dental leaders were too engrossed in removing tartar, filling holes in teeth, performing extractions and making dentures, and the concept of killing the microorganisms associated with disease fell by the wayside.

No history would be complete without a discussion of Willoughby Dayton Miller (1853-1907), the first dentist in history with a complete training in the natural sciences. After studying mathematics and physics at the University of Ann Arbor, Michigan, from 1871-1875, Miller planned to pursue additional courses in Europe. Unfortunately, while studying in Edinburgh, his bank went bankrupt and he lost nearly all of his money. It was only through the acquaintance of Frank Abbot, an American dentist practicing in Berlin, that Miller was able to continue his studies. Dr. Abbot found him a job as a translator and asked that he give math lessons to his wife and daughter. How much the ladies actually learned from Miller is unknown, because Miller soon became engaged to marry Miss Caroline Abbot, the daughter. He also began to favor his future father-in-law's profession. With the support of this generous man, Miller returned to the United States to study dentistry.

After graduating from Philadelphia Dental College in 1879, Miller returned to Berlin to assist in his father-in-law's practice. Continuing to study, he developed an interest in Microbiology, a field which had just made enormous progress under the influence of world renown Dr. Robert Koch. Dr. Koch had recently written a paper that would serve as the framework for modern microbiology. The famous Koch's Postulates, simply stated, said that in order for a bacterium to be proven the cause for a particular disease, the following criteria must be met: 1) the suspected bacterium must be isolated and grown in pure culture; 2) the isolate must be inoculated into a susceptible animal model; 3 the clinical symptoms of the disease must be present in the animal model; 4) the suspected bacterium must, again, be isolated from the diseased animal and grown in culture.

Koch's methods appealed greatly to the research-minded Miller. Dr. Miller was a very hard worker and he attacked the mysteries of dental diseases with such a thoroughness and versatility of methods that must still amaze the most sophisticated researcher today. Between 1881 and 1907, Miller published 164 scientific articles in German, American and English journals. His most famous work was a book first published in Germany in 1889 titled "Die Mirooganismen der Mundhohle." The better known English version is called "The Microorganisms of the Human Mouth" printed in Philadelphia a year after the German original.

An outstanding histopathologist, the results of his investigations of decay and the infections of the pulp (nerve) were a step from the stone age to modern science. The vicinity of Miller's small laboratory to Robert Koch's Institute (about two city blocks) obviously influenced his perception of microbiology. His book is most famous for its chapter on the cause of dental decay where he describes two factors in the decay process—the action of acids and the action of germs. Miller had an unbelievable comprehension of the possibility for the prevention of decay. His statements are as valid today as they were then when he writes, "We may endeavor 1) by hygienic measures to secure the best possible development of the teeth; 2) by repeated thorough systematic cleansing of the oral cavity and the teeth to so-far reduce the amount of fermentable bacteria of organic matter necessary to their rapid development; 3) by prohibiting or limiting the consumption of such foods or luxuries which readily undergo acid fermentation to remove the chief source of ferment products injurious to the teeth; 4) by the proper and intelligent use of antiseptics to destroy the bacteria or at least limit their number and activity."

During this period, a famous dentist in America, G.V. Black, and a colleague, J.L. Williams, were describing the cause of caries as being from "plaque" and they criticized Miller for his so-called misconception of the etiologic or causative role of plaque. Miller persisted in failing to recognize the term plaque, but in 1902 he bowed to the pressure of his "more learned colleagues" and published an article titled, "The Presence of

Bacterial Plaque on the Surfaces of Teeth and Their Significance," which appeared in *Dental Cosmos*, May, 1902. The article begins with a defense that Miller had previously recognized plague, citing earlier quotations from his writings where he has pointed out masses of bacteria in a matrix on a tooth surface. But the matrix he refers to was the protein pellicle sticking to the tooth enamel which is thickened and invaded by masses of bacteria. Miller then enlarged on Williams' opinion that all enamel softening in the decay process is due only to the action of acids chiefly coming from bacterial excretions within the plaque.

This disagreement between the scientists was so crucial to subsequent history of oral microbiology that it retarded the profession's ability to deal with dental infections until today. It is the basic difference between my concepts and those of the majority of dentistry. Williams believed that the type of bacteria did not matter as all were just normal inhabitants, only when plaque formed were acids concentrated. So the target became plaque and the best way to attack plaque was to clean it. This mentality was quickly adopted by the mechanically-minded dentists who saw their role as helping patients remove plaque and tartar.

Miller also made the mistake of assuming that the bacteria associated with gum disease and caries were normal inhabitants of the mouth. If we observe the process in medicine as it conquered other bacterial infections, we can only thank God they did not follow dentistry's lead. For a while, bacteria such as the tubercle bacillus that causes tuberculosis was considered a normal inhabitant of the mouth and Strep throat (caused by Strep. pyogenes) was thought to be more of a problem with the person's own constitution than a specific infection. Fortunately, medicine changed and attempted to eliminate the disease associated bacteria, and cases of TB, scarlet fever, and rheumatic fever are no longer major threats. Dental infections could easily follow the same course.

I am most fascinated in reading Dr. Miller's book. Even though it was written in 1897 it is amazingly accurate and served as a benchmark for all future books on Oral Microbiology. In fact, when I read a modern text, it almost appears they have just plagiarized much of Miller's work. His descriptions of noxious bacteria are incredible given his crude microscopes and culturing capabilities. His description of the bacteria associated with periodontal disease does not differ very much from how I would describe them today. It is easy to understand why he made his mistake in terms of the "normal bacteria theory," because every patient he saw had the same bacteria (they all had gum disease). But this mistake or capitulation to his American colleagues has caused the normal flora theory to become so rooted in the minds of dentists that it seems almost impossible to remove.

The mistake that it is only a cleaning problem intertwines and permeates all parts of the modern dental practice. We have created an army of hygienists and dentists busily scraping, drilling or cutting. Let's fantasize a nightmare:

In 1940 the prevalence of Tuberculosis led to a floor fight at the annual meeting of the American Medical Association. The thoracic surgeons were successful in their bid to take control of the treatment of TB. It was argued that because the bacteria causing TB are normal inhabitants of everybody's respiratory system it really is more of a cleaning problem. The surgeons have invented a series of instruments that will allow them to brush many of the lesions close to the main bronchia. They hope to have a home use model in the near future. However, many lesions cannot be reached in this fashion requiring surgery where the lungs are opened and scraped directly. Since that time, the surgeons have worked relentlessly to reduce the number of failed cases. Although one study in 1981 claimed only twenty seven per cent of the cases treated surgically showed complete remission for a five year period, many claim far greater success. There has been much hope placed on new synthetic materials to take the place of missing lung tissue and the material, Goretex, is now being touted as the best material to stimulate the body to form new lung tissue. This material is first placed after careful surgery to remove all diseased tissue. After four weeks, the patient is again surgerized and the material carefully removed. There is evidence that some new lung tissue can be stimulated to form. The thoracic surgeons are vehemently opposed to the use of antimicrobial agents as they claim not enough proof has been presented.

Although the above is not true, substituting periodontal disease for TB describes basically what has happened in dentistry. But dentistry has always had leaders that were opposed to the mechanical methods.

C.C. Bass, a physician who was Dean of Tulane Medical School, Thomas B. Hartzell, and others did not agree. Bass wrote in the early 1900's about the need for microscopic examinations and identifying specific microbial targets. But he could not even get his writings published in the Journals controlled by the American Dental Association. Thomas B. Hartzell fought all his professional life for conservative, antimicrobial approaches to gum disease and, although he was a renowned physician and dentist who actually became one of the first periodontal specialists and started the school of Periodontology at the University of Minnesota, his colleagues would not listen. In his final address to the Academy of Periodontology in 1940, he said:

"The dearest wish of my life would be gratified if I could convince members of this Academy that the use of the principles laid down by Pasteur, would tremendously enhance the success of the conscientious periodontist: because it would be as impossible for pyorrhea to exist in the tissues around human teeth were it not for the invasion of pus germs growing on the sides of the teeth, as it would be to harvest wheat if we did not first plant wheat." No one has ever said it more succinctly!

The mechanical-minded dentists though were too comfortable with the hygiene theory and fought the likes of Bass and Hartzell. Bass never got anything published outside Louisiana except for his treatise on toothbrushing, which has become the *standard* way patients are taught to brush. The "Bass Technique" is taught by almost every dental hygiene school.

Naturally, politics came into play and the mechanics used their majority to force a statement from the American Dental Association's Council on Dental Therapeutics. Written below is the statement as it appeared from the Council in the dental handbook, *ACCEPTED DENTAL REMEDIES:*

"Dentifrices are defined as preparations (pastes, powders, and liquids) which aid in the removal of debris from the tooth surface.

Tooth pastes and powders on the market today may in general be placed in several different groups or combinations of groups: namely, those depending primarily on soap for their cleaning action: those containing small amounts of organic acids: those containing magnesia magma or other alkaline substances, enzymes, etc. These substances are generally mixed with chalk for abrasive action and incorporated in paste form by glycerol(or glycerite or starch), tragacantin, acacia or other pharmaceutical binders.

Many dentifrices on the market today are unnecessarily and irrationally complex in composition. The Council desires to point out that the aims of rational therapeutics and oral hygiene are defeated by the use of complex mixtures, not to mention the large economic waste in the sale of highly complex materials when simpler combinations are just as effective. This is in keeping with the well known observation that dentifrices have no direct demonstrable therapeutic action. *The sole function of a dentifrice is to aid in keeping the teeth clean by the removal of loose food debris by the mechanical use of the toothbrush."*

This was really too bad because at the time (1920's) there were several toothpastes or dentifrices with some therapeutic benefit—products like Kolynos toothpaste, Dr. Lyons and Pycopay tooth powders. But the toothpaste manufacturers found that it was more profitable to put abrasives, sweeteners, and taste pleasers in their toothpastes, so all the beneficial dentifrices died out and interest in the disease process remained quiet until the 1950's.

Meanwhile, the dental profession continued to hone its mechanical skills. Periodontists in the 1940's increased the use of surgical procedures to cut back the diseased gum tissue. It was concluded that the periodontal pocket (that space formed between the tooth and the gum by disease) was really the culprit and a surgical method was devised to trim away all unattached gum tissue. It was also felt that any concave areas or divots in the bone should be removed. This led to a procedure called a gingivectomy with ramping of bone using large chiropodist burs. Many people were prematurely made "long in the tooth" with this procedure, but by eliminating the pocket, periodontal disease was at least slowed. There were many side effects, however, and many patients complained of sensitivity due to the exposed tooth roots and the unsightly appearance. A large percentage of patients refused to have the procedure done, and many who did returned to their general dentist saying, "Please don't send me there again! I would rather lose my teeth than repeat that surgery."

Many schools of dentistry refused to teach the surgical approach. The Medical College of Virginia did not allow a scalpel in their periodontal department while Dr. Harry Lyons was chairman (which was quite a while). Others were just as adamant so a distrust grew between the general dentist and the surgically oriented periodontist.

In the 1970's a German researcher, named Waerhaug, wrote many papers stating that simple root planing did not remove all the calculus and demonstrated it by removing previously scaled teeth. Since it was generally accepted at this time that calculus was the cause of disease, he concluded that once a gum pocket became deeper that four millimeters it could only be treated surgically. He and other researchers developed less invasive surgical techniques and the sophistication of the periodontist was off and running. They refined their surgical procedures and developed highly technical miniature tissue and bone grafting techniques. Many periodontists continued to treat their patients with conservative root planing, using surgery only for those areas that did not properly heal. Others justified surgery because it produced results more quickly than the more time consuming root planing. Still others felt Waerhaug's work justified surgery for any gum pocket over three millimeters deep. Periodontists were also frustrated that referral from the general dentists was not timely, as few G.P.'s recognized gum disease until significant bone loss had occurred. They became bolder and began admonishing their general dentist colleagues for not referring patients with early signs of disease. They often badgered G.P.'s and let it be known that they were on shaky legal ground if they tried to treat the patients themselves. The American Academy of Periodontology even initiated a nation-wide television campaign to alert the public that if they noticed signs of gums disease: bleeding, bad breath, pain, etc., they should go directly to their periodontist, thus circumventing the normal referral routine. Most general dentists were upset with these tactics, but felt inadequate to challenge the knowledge of the periodontist. Besides, there were enough restorative problems to deal with without arguing over periodontal care.

Far removed from the mainstream of dental practice, researchers were making headway into the causes of dental diseases. In 1960, the primary cause of caries was identified as Streptococcus mutans and was shown to be transmissible in hamsters. Other studies revealed the effects of fluoride on preventing decay. Procter and Gamble introduced Crest toothpaste. So powerful was this new data that the federal government began an energetic program of fluoridation of city waters throughout the country. One would think that such an impact of one chemical antimicrobial agent would have stimulated more interest in the bacteria causing periodontal diseases, but such thinking was limited to a very few.

One such person, Walter Loesche, head of the Oral Microbiology department at the University of Michigan School of Dentistry, proposed the **Specific Plaque Theory** stating that all dental plaques were specific in their microbial make-up and varied between those producing disease and those maintaining health.

This means we needed to find ways to identify those plaques that caused disease.

Working on gum disease at the National Institutes of Health, Dr. Paul Keyes, was thinking along the same lines as Dr. Loesche. He observed many patients over forty-five years of age with no sign of ever having gum disease and they exhibited a distinct pattern of bacteria observed under a phase contrast microscope. He then examined patients with obvious active gum disease and noted that the patterns of bacteria were quite different. Large motile bacteria were always present in the diseased patients and they showed a discernably higher white blood cell count.

He asked himself what would happen if he used antimicrobial agents and changed the bacterial patterns of the diseased patients to look like the patterns observed in the healthy patients. He established a long term study where large motile microorganisms (spirochetes, gliding rods, spinning rods, amoebae, trichomonads, eel-like forms, etc. ) were targeted for elimination. He found that these organisms were sensitive to simple salts and, because they cannot live in the presence of oxygen, peroxide. He also found that it was very helpful to break up the thick mats of organisms by careful scaling. Sometimes antibiotics were needed and he used tetracycline. As his study progressed, he found that, with perseverance and the patients' help, most patients in the study were converted to a health related microbial flora, and everyone of those converted exhibited no signs of disease. He was amazed at the tremendous healing in the converted patients—far greater than anything previously reported in the dental literature.

Paul was fairly blunt in his conversations with fellow researchers who could not believe his results were that good. There was a consensus that Paul really was not on to anything meaningful; besides how could they justify spending precious research monies on baking soda and peroxide? He received little personnel support and was not consulted when an independent study was contracted at an outside university to evaluate his work. It seemed that this maverick was tolerated because of his senior status.

Despite these handicaps, Paul managed to follow over 150 patients between 1975 and 1981 gathering a tremendous amount of data. Many of the patients had been referred to NIH as a last resort and had previously been treated surgically. It was astonishing to see bone growing back around the teeth and many became perfectly firm, even though they were on the verge of falling out before treatment was initiated. He tried to publish his first paper on the subject in 1978, but was thwarted by Journal referees who said his work "was not scientific enough." It seemed as though the scientific community was not happy with Paul's methods, agents, or him.

About this time a health science journalist found out that she had advanced gum disease and a visit to a periodontist produced a treatment plan that included about $4,000 worth of surgery. Being an investigative reporter, she nosed around and found Paul Keyes. After a couple of months of simple treatment, she was cured, healed and angry! She wrote an article that appeared in **MODERN MATURITY** magazine. The telephones at NIH were flooded with calls from people suffering the same fate as the reporter. This made the dental scientific community furious because researchers are never supposed to go to the press. Thus, the controversy was born.

I had run across Paul in 1978 and spent time with him, observing several of his patients under treatment. With my undergraduate major in microbiology, his methods seemed right on target. After purchasing a microscope and gaining several successful treatments on my own, I became so enthusiastic that promoting this rationale became an obsession.

I was getting fantastic results, but several issues still bothered me. Where did these bacteria actually come from and how do we know what is optimum health associated bacterial flora? To find these answers, I perused many microbiology textbooks. Most authors were as in the dark as I was but a few insights were gleaned. First of all, there are many times more bacteria living in the G.I. (Gastro Intestinal) tract (from mouth to anus, thank God we do not have a high incidence of disease treated by surgeons at that end!) than there are cells in the body, which means that these ecosystems have far more to do with our general health then anyone realizes. I am sure that there is an optimum flora and then several less than optimum floras that can influence how we feel. They may make the difference between excellent health and fair health. They may play a part in whether we feel great or just so. They may contribute to a host of illnesses that do not produce outright symptoms but make us sustain less than perfect health. It is possible that such conditions contribute to some of the chronic degenerative diseases; such as, arthritis, diabetes, kidney, and liver diseases. It is also quite possible that our own actions contribute to these floras in what we eat, drink smoke, and become exposed to from other persons. I predict that twenty-first century medicine will find, by monitoring and changing these microbial ecosystems, that health and longevity will be enhanced.

When we are born we have no bacteria in our G.I. tract, but by the second month, our own flora is developing. Obviously, the likely source of these germs is from our caretakers as all babies like putting their fingers into mouths, etc. In a sense it is another form of inheritance, especially from our mothers. As the population grows, each species of organisms compete for turf. Illnesses affect winners and losers, along with ingested food, our own immune systems and contact with strangers (nurseries, etc.) The outcome is that each of us has similar bacterial patterns, especially in those patterns capable of aiding our protection against harmful invaders. We need these microbes to survive, yet our understanding of their specific roles remains a mystery.

Observing the bacteria associated with gum disease reveals a family of organisms with definite characteristics. They belong to a group that will stain red when a gram stain is applied (as opposed to others that stain blue). This family is generally less sensitive to penicillin-type antibiotics and tends to be more adversely affected by oxygen. It seems that the more motile forms, such as spirochetes, are easily killed by oxygen and, therefore, can only survive in an oxygen free environment. Obviously, we cannot catch them from the air, and their metabolic requirements are so fastidious that it is only logical that they are passed from person to person through the transmission of saliva. This hypothesis is once again borne out when we observe diseases caused by similar bacteria - syphilis and other venereal diseases, plus those passed by the bite of a tick. Knowing these things helped Paul and I enjoy greater and greater success with our treatment.

When Paul retired in 1981 (there was a TV brief featuring Paul being cast out of NIH on Walter Cronkite's short lived hour news show), he and I formed the International Dental Health Foundation. How naive I was to think all we needed to do was get the word out to the practicing dentists and they would embrace the rationale as quickly and enthusiastically as I did.

We started a lecture series visiting several cities with a one day presentation. Paul gave the theory and background and I related how it could be set up in a private practice. The response of many periodontists was incredible! Many times a small group of specialists would come to our seminar just to heckle, sneer and exclaim that we were the "laetrile of dentistry." They were most upset with our non- surgical approach, although we did not rule out surgery, but placed it as a last resort. They laughed at the thought of using antimicrobial agents. Such actions only strengthened our resolve.

We increased our seminars and over the next two years we lectured in 120 cities. Our backgrounds gave us synergy as Paul's vast scientific background did not include private clinical practice and I was able to make his information meaningful to the average dentist. We developed a **Seven Step System** for disease management and started a membership in the Foundation and a Newsletter.

There was great clamor among the dental scientific community. Five dental school periodontal departments completed studies that concluded our technique was no better than traditional care. When one scrutinized these studies it was clear that they did not follow our complete system. Basically, they were measuring the bacteria in deep gum pockets and not delivering agents into these pockets. A similar study would be to rub penicillin on the chest to see if it would affect pneumonia. As demonstrated in the next chapter, another important part of the **Seven Step System** clearly explains that when a patient returns with active disease we change our treatment procedures until we eliminate the disease-associated bacteria, which was not done in the studies.

These studies did accomplish one thing, however. The press had picked up on our work and articles began appearing in most major magazines. The articles generally missed some vital points of our system, concentrating rather on extolling the benefits of brushing with baking soda and peroxide. The studies showed that people could not treat themselves exclusively without the help of a professional because it is necessary to deliver the antimicrobial correctly to the infected site. Simple brushing with baking soda and peroxide will not reach into pockets that have already formed, so the studies were right that the news articles were misleading when they suggested that such simple procedures could heal those with advanced disease.

Although several periodontists came to our courses with open minds and found our methods extremely beneficial to their patients, many continued to be hostile. In certain areas all the local periodontists signed letters to the general dentists warning them not to embrace our treatment system or suffer legal ramifications. The A.A.P. formed a "blue ribbon" panel of experts who came to Washington and examined Paul's research data. Even though the experts were denied access to the actual patient charts, they found "discrepancies" in the computer data and the protocol. The A.A.P. published a position paper that basically said his work was flawed.

In 1986, however, a person became President of the American Academy of Periodontology who saw the need to heal the wounds between general dentists and periodontists. He also was not totally closed-minded about the use of antimicrobials and we began to move closer together. His successors have continued this direction. There are many scientific articles in the Dental Journals these days concerning antimicrobials and non-surgical therapy. We still see a different picture, but the hostilities are subsiding and we are coming closer in our treatment rationale.

Highlights of three of these scientific articles should be of interest to you as they add tremendous credibility to our way of thinking. The first is an article by Harold Loe, the Director of the National Institute of Dental Research, titled **PERIODON-TOLOGY IN THE PAST TWENTY YEARS,** Danish Dental Journal, June, 1986.

"It is no exaggeration to say that the discovery that the human periodontal diseases were infectious disorders caused a major change in their clinical management. . ."

"Occlusal (biting) disharmonies and dysfunction have been shown *not* to produce gingivitis or periodontitis."

". . .it follows that an effective prevention of gingivitis will prevent the development of periodontitis as well."

"It is now 15 years since we in Aarhus (Norway) revived the utility of general antiseptics and antimicrobials in the prevention of periodontitis and caries. . . To make a long story short; it is now quite clear on the basis of more than one thousand scientific papers and 15 years of clinical experience, that chlorhexidine is one of the most effective antiseptics known and the side-effects are minimal and without real consequence."

"The studies . . . have shown . . . that whether the competent clinician treats the advanced (gum) lesion surgically or non-surgically really makes no difference."

". . .it is probably fair to say that new attachment

procedures (bone grafting,etc. ) continue to be essentially unpredictable. . ."

"Both the image and substance of periodontology have changed during the last 20 years and significant progress in the clinical management of periodontal diseases has occurred."

Another landmark article appeared in the Journal of Periodontal Research in 1987, titled **HIGHLIGHTS OF THE CONFERENCE AND PERSPECTIVES FOR THE FUTURE,** by Dr. Robert Genco, Department of Oral Biology and Periodontal Research Center, State University of New York at Buffalo. This was an overview of a conference of leading dental researchers in dental diseases.

"We are now making a transition from the **Endogenous Infection Era** to the **Exogenous Infection Era** since some of the specific organisms we now associate with periodontal infections are not widely distributed in the normal oral flora. . .

The exogenous infection theory has implications with respect to treatment. Theoretically, it should be easier to eradicate and eliminate organisms which are normally not established members of the oral flora. Furthermore, their presence would indicate either a carrier state or progressive disease and hence microbiological tests which they were detected would be readily interpretable . . . The objective of therapy would then be to eliminate the organism and, indeed, this could be carried out by elimination of the organism at the periodontal site, the whole oral cavity, and even in families where the organism may be carried and transmitted from person to person."

"We learned from . . . long-term studies comparing various surgical techniques with scaling and root planing that, in the deeper pockets there was no significant advantage of one technique over another . . .
     An interesting aspect . . . there is significant bone loss after periodontal surgery . . ."
"We have passed from the **Era of Resective Therapy to the Era of Anti-infective Therapy.** Resective therapy was designed to eliminate gingival or periodontal pockets by gingivectomy and various flap procedures and to eliminate . . . infrabony defects . . . Future investigations, I predict, will firmly establish that anti-infective therapy is the principal means of treatment of periodontal diseases."
"Periodontal diseases are clearly infections . . ."
     The last article is a paper presented by Dr. Walter Loesche titled **BACTERIAL PROFILES OF SUB-GINGIVAL PLAQUES IN PERIODONTITIS** published in 1985 in the Journal of Periodontology.
     "The data indicate that the various types of periodontitis with the possible exception of LJP (a rare juvenile form) are specific anaerobic infections involving spirochetes and to a lesser extent . . ." (other bacteria)

As a student of dental research literature, it is beyond me that such writings could be ignored by mainstream practitioners. These researchers are very closely in line with the thinking we incorporated in our treatment, so really there is very little controversy.

Over the years, we have continued to change agents and methods as newer ideas are advanced, but this fits easily into our treatment concept. I am constantly trying something new and change in a heartbeat if there is clearly a better way to treat.

The membership in the International Dental Health Foundation has grown and the member clinicians have been just as enthusiastic because of their success in treating patients. These clinicians are a joy to know and I am convinced they are the finest dentistry has to offer. That is the bottom line and, as I say in my lecture, if one patient benefits, it makes our efforts worthwhile.

A closer look at the modern dentist may clarify our understanding.

# Chapter 8
# THE MODERN DENTAL PRACTICE

I majored in Microbiology at Ohio State University. Upon entering OSU Dental School in 1963, the faculty advisor informed me that with my undergraduate major I did not need to take the freshman course in Oral Microbiology. I responded that we really had not studied the oral microflora and he said, "Well, it really doesn't make much difference." The profession was still inundated with damage from dental diseases and the highest priority was definitely placed on learning how to repair. It is obvious that we still have a long way to go.

During my four years of dental training, we spent very little time learning about disease management. We were not even well informed on the mechanisms of fluoride's ability to prevent decay. Much time was spent on Anatomy, Pathology, Histology, etc. , which made us very good at describing what was present in the mouth (this is a typical method of training surgeons). Other courses in medicine were taught in cookbook style—to be memorized and soon forgotten. Even today only about 160 hours out of a possible 6000 hours of dental training are devoted to the entire spectrum of periodontal diseases.

The largest and most powerful department in the school was Prosthetics, that part of dentistry concerned with dentures. We labored many hours over the construction of metal partial dentures and full dentures. It was an underlying feeling among students in this department that the loss of teeth was inevitable for most people and so they should devote the majority of their time learning the skills of denture making.

As my dental class approached graduation in 1967, we were faced with unprecedented uncertainties. The Vietnam war was in full swing and most of us already were committed to military service or would soon be drafted. Until now graduating dentists had few concerns. There existed an overwhelming number of damaged teeth and all a new dentist had to do was decide where he wanted to practice and hang out his shingle. Banks would loan any D.D.S. money even if his pockets were empty, because everyone knew that dentists were going to be successful, and money was the measure of success. The amount of success was dependent upon one's ability to "sell" expensive dentistry and the speed by which it was delivered. Generally, it was not the most gifted students who gained the greatest financial success but those in the class who were better salesmen than scientists.

Conversations among my classmates, though, included more than just the problem with the war. We had heard new data that showed fluorides in toothpastes and drinking water were greatly affecting the decay rate. Our professors reassured us that there were still so many damaged teeth out there that we really need not worry. They estimated it would take at least fifty years to catch up. There was much talk about how to convince the fifty per cent of the population who did not visit the dentist regularly to start doing so. The profession was convinced that there were vast numbers of cavities in the mouths of people who would not seek regular dental care, mostly out of fear or ignorance. The secret was to convince enough people to become regular patients. I remember visiting the practice of one instructor who was regarded as successful. His formula was to gain a patient population of three thousand, not to try to sell them everything at once, but sell them something every time they came in for a recall visit. In other words, get out the active decay and then "plant the seeds" for the need for crowns, bridges, etc. in the future. He felt that it would take him twenty years to complete all the work on the patients in his practice. Then he could provide dentures for those who lost their teeth.

A graduating dentist has very little business training. No part of dental education deals with practice management and the fledgling dentist receives on the job training in accounting, personnel management, trends within the practice, etc. This is not an insurmountable problem when the patients are flocking into the waiting room and most of my classmates learned by their own mistakes. So we ventured out into private practice with our heads chocked full of technical procedures, not even knowing how to hire a staff. In short, we were technicians who had learned to identify and fix certain defects but not how to deal with deviations. We were well trained but not well taught.

Although there were flaws in dental training, dentists were doing a marvelous job for their patients.

The emphasis was on quality work for a quality price. This was the "Golden Age" of dentistry and average income for practicing dentists continued to rise. There were more and more people who had grown up in households that could not afford optimum dentistry, but were now affluent enough to afford at least some crown and bridge work. It was a time when the rigors of providing highly demanding technical procedures hour after hour with never wavering perfection raised the suicide rate among dentists to the highest among professions.

Upon my return from Vietnam, I was informed of my selection for Ohio State Dental School's Oral Surgery Program. Quite an honor considering they only accepted three out of a reported two hundred applicants. Due to the fact that Vietnam had thrust me into many surgical situations and I did not wish to submit my family to further sacrifice, I turned it down. Many classmates, however, opted for graduate training in the specialties. Many instructors of these specialties taught undergraduate dental courses on their respective topics and many times taught the aspiring general dentists only enough to recognize the need for care and when to refer the patient to a specialist. This was considered a turf protection measure to discourage general dentists from trying to treat their own cases. Orthodontics and Periodontics have often been considered the greatest offenders, leaving a constant source of contention between the specialists of these two areas and the general dentists.

Periodontists had a legitimate gripe. Many general practitioners (G.P.'s) were not examining their patients for gum disease until one day a tooth would loosen or ache and the G.P. would note advanced gum problems and refer to the periodontist. Patients would wonder how they could be suffering from an advanced condition since they had been regularly visiting the G.P. A large percentage of referrals were in this category and periodontists were worn down trying to bail out the general dentist. Remember the Iowa study that showed that the incidence of periodontal diseases is as high in populations that seek regular dental care as those who do not.

To become a periodontist, a dentist must be accepted into a two year graduate program. The vast majority of training in these programs is learning to apply highly sophisticated and technical surgical procedures to correct the defects caused by periodontal diseases. Great satisfaction is obtained by mastering these intricate procedures and, no doubt, most periodontists are highly skilled surgeons. They like to view themselves as the "plastic surgeons of the mouth." You can imagine how disturbing it would be to sacrifice two more years, limit practice to periodontics, invest in a practice, build up a lucrative business and then have someone come along and say most surgery is not necessary. There are many periodontists who agree with our concepts and practice with a philosophy similar to mine. But I am afraid that an alarming percentage are vehemently opposed to changing from a surgical approach. Daily, patients come to my office seeking second opinions because of the treatment plans offered by specialists, and they are not being offered any treatment except surgery.

Many post graduate courses were developed to help the general dentist in practice management. Courses taught dentists that every patient could afford optimum dentistry once they properly ordered their priorities. After all, wasn't a pretty smile and a perfect bite as important as driving a new car? We just needed to teach patients how to reshuffle their priority list. Such practice management courses dominate post graduate training available to the practicing clinician. For a healthy fee, dental gurus will come into an office, analyze the books and tell a dentist how to increase monthly gross income. One common measure was the percentage of crown and bridge work completed by the practice. If a dental office was under the "acceptable" per cent, the guru would spend much of the day telling you how to better "sell" crowns and bridges. I have a grave problem with salesmanship being exhorted by almost every dental teaching institution as it compels the practicing dentist to sell dentistry rather than evaluate the patient's *need*. During the late seventies, most practices began to feel the declining decay rate and patient awareness of their needs increased. The "busyness" problem was being discussed by the American Dental Association. The Association decided to spend over a million dollars in advertising to reach that population group which did not seek regular visits. The message was the same as ever, "Brush three times a day, floss daily, and visit your dentist every six months."

Dentists began to look harder at the problems that provide greater economic return. A few years ago, the most predominant short courses offered to dentists concerned the jaw joint, professionally known as the Temporal-mandibular Joint or TMJ. It was the "in" disease. Dozens of "experts" travelled from city to city teaching local dentists their methods. TMJ Dysfunction, as it is called became a dental buzzword with many dentists vying for recognition as an expert. The problem is that such a small percentage of the population has a true TMJ Dysfunction, and this has led to misdiagnosis of many cases as clinicians seek to use their newfound expertise and stretch marginal symptoms into full blown problems. The television program, **20/20,** recently looked into TMJ treatment and interviewed a number of patients that had spent thousands of dollars with little improvement. So even those with true TMJ syndrome cannot always find proper help.

Implant dentistry is another area where numerous courses are offered and dentists are flocking in to learn the intricate, but costly, procedures. These dentists believe that if they could find just a dozen implant cases a year they could solve their "busyness problems." Although many dentists have toiled very hard to educate themselves to become true experts in implant treatment, the process is complex and there is risk that overzealous dentists might take a short course and begin marketing implants to their patients without the proper skill. Don't get me wrong, there are excellent clinicians providing needy patients with marvelous implants, but it does require considerable expertise. I am concerned that all those offering such treatment do not have such expertise and may do more harm than good.

The dental trade newspapers bombard dentists with ways to motivate patients and gain greater financial rewards. Just recently, I read an article in a trade newspaper on how to motivate the patient to accept treatment for periodontal disease. The author wrote, "I train doctors and staff to practice specific scripts of the message so they are able to deliver it when they do the patient consultations." If a clinician needs a script, I doubt his/her ability to properly assess and re-assess a patient through the complicated periodontal treatment process.

The dental hygienist is a position created to aid patients in prevention of dental diseases by professional cleanings. The problem, however, is that the majority of patients already have disease and hygienists spin their wheels trying to prevent something that is already there. For years hygienists have campaigned for more authority to provide treatment which resulted in most states allowing hygienists to perform deep scalings.

This has helped but many deep seated problems exist. Historically, dentists have been wary of the hygienists gaining too much authority and undermining the current structure of practice. Many dentists enjoy sloughing off disease management to the hygienist, but they want total control. A recent legal case points this out very well. The dentist had seen a patient for six years, during which time the patient had developed severe periodontal disease, losing one tooth and many others were in jeopardy. He had relied on his hygienist to provide the treatment and even chart the cavities. Many times he did not even see the patient when she came in for her semi-annual visits. When the patient began complaining about pain and a foul breath, the dentist fired the hygienist and scaled the patient's teeth himself. He insisted that the problem lay entirely with the patient's home care and had she brushed properly and had the hygienist been monitoring her brushing, there would be no problem. He claimed that he knew the patient wasn't brushing properly because after he started seeing her, her gums would still bleed when she came in (which was still only every six months). The interesting part of this is that the hygienist by law is forbidden to diagnose and direct treatment.

So the poor hygienist was strapped with unlawful responsibility and yet had to follow the procedures dictated by the dentist for whom she worked. There are other complicating factors, but this points out the main reason why hygienists are fighting for independent practice and more authority. Organized hygiene has clouded the picture by highlighting economic issues, rather than treatment issues.

The dental hygienist is in the best position to provide almost all disease management. Their training already involves ten times more hours in periodontal treatment than does the training for a D.D.S. degree and they are in tune with the need to actually treat disease. All they need is to beef up their knowledge in infectious diseases and microbiology.

There is a serious problem rising for dental hygiene. The interest in dental hygiene as a career has dwindled and applications for positions in schools have dropped off precipitously. This has caused an urgent demand for hygienists and new graduates are being offered lucrative salaries as offices compete for their services. In many practices, the hygiene department has gone from a profit center to a loss leader. Dental societies around the country have addressed this problem and the solution most often mentioned is to allow a dental assistant to become certified as a hygienist by completing a two week preceptorship in a recognized dental practice. If this happens it will a *major disaster* and set dentistry back thirty years.

Another large problem is already on the scene that virtually changed the lives of the entire dental profession—dental insurance. This monster slowly changed from an aid for the poorer patient to a menacing giant dictating how dental care is to be delivered. It seemed so good for the dentist in the beginning because we would not need to hassle with patients' financial problems and the patients with major problems could gain financial assistance. It quickly became the darling of unions as it was used as a bargaining chip during contract negotiations. The insurance companies saw many dollars to be made in the dental health arena and analyzed how their programs could produce the highest profits.

The mentality of insurance companies is best understood by relating my experience speaking to the Health Insurance Association. This is a non-profit organization with members from all insurance companies providing health care insurance. The Board of Directors consists of the top ten providers (I'll leave the function of this organization to your imagination). They invited me to speak to the Board about our rationale of treatment. Being naive, I thought this was our big chance to show them how our treatment was far better and less costly than what they were currently paying for. I got into a good speaking rhythm and thought they were grasping how much more effective our approach is when one fellow raised his hand and said "Dr. Watt, I don't wish to sound crass, but in actuality we really don't care if your treatment is better for the patient. It is not our job to pass judgment on the quality of treatment, but to sell coverage that companies and patients will buy. If they want coverage for periodontal surgery, we need to provide it at a competitive price."

Dental insurance differs from medical insurance because many people seeking coverage have a definite problem, where people seeking medical insurance are mainly healthy and want coverage in the unlikely event that they become ill. Further analysis of dental insurance reveals that the party that is really being insured is *the insurance company*. An expert will tell you that the only reason for insurance is to avoid large or catastrophic losses. Most dental insurance plans decrease their coverage as the cost of a given treatment goes up. In other words, the plans pay well for simple procedures, but if you break a tooth and need a root canal or a crown, generally the percentage of payment is drastically reduced. So who is being protected against catastrophic losses?! Dental insurance really has become a fringe benefit where the idea is to get the most amount of dental work for the least amount of dollar input.

This kind of mentality has changed the basic

framework of the dental practice. Insurance companies began this change by implementing the ninety per cent rule. This rule states that payment for services will be based on ninety percent of the usual and customary fees in a given geographic area. It doesn't take a whiz to figure out that not only do you lose ten percent this time, but next time the fee will be ninety percent of ninety percent and so on. Insurance companies further harass clinicians by singling out a dentist who is performing more than the average of any one procedure. God forbid if you are not average!

Then came the HMO's (health maintenance organizations) and PPO's (preferred provider organizations). These inventions may have a place in medicine, but they have wreaked havoc in dentistry. The problem is different. In medicine, the idea is that you join one of these organizations in a relatively healthy state and they will maintain you for a set monthly fee. In dentistry, however, the person interested in such a plan generally needs complex treatment and has put it off because of cost, and he sees this as a way of getting the work for a much reduced fee. After the work is completed, this patient will leave the plan and the dentist winds up providing expensive procedures at greatly reduced fees.

One last thought on dental insurance, the insurance companies make about thirty percent of every dollar spent for dental care under their coverage. Someone has to pay them—you, your employer, other people in the plan, or the dentist.

No doubt that the declining decay rate has increased competition among practitioners for patients.

The insurance companies have capitalized on this by providing patients for reduced fees. The dentists have responded by creating clinics where patients can be treated more rapidly and efficiently. Production has become the dominant priority making dental service nothing more than a commodity, and we practitioners feel that professionalism is going by the wayside.

It used to be that dentists took great pride in their work, but pride has to give way to profit margins and time constraints. Now, the definition of quality seems to be what you can get away with and not get into legal trouble. This is not universal and many practitioners, including myself, fight hard to still use only the best materials and insist on only the highest technical standards. But it is difficult knowing that some of our colleagues are reaping higher profits by only performing the most cost effective treatment and that their way is promoted by insurance.

I am reminded of a segment in early 1988 of the TV show, **SIXTY MINUTES,** where several clinics in California were being exposed for their alleged lack of quality. One such clinic was questioned because they did their diagnosis strictly by x-ray and figured out just what it would take to get payment for expensive procedures by the insurance company. The interviewer attempted to paint a dismal picture of the clinic's owner, but one must sympathize with him because he was strictly playing the game in the same manner as the insurance company. For example, most insurance companies require approval for all dental work over a minimum dollar figure. This is accomplished by requesting x-rays and a treatment plan be sent to the company prior to starting the work. This procedure is called a "pre-authorization." The company has its dentist advisor look at the x-rays to see if he agrees with the proposed treatment; in other words, the company can diagnose what they think should be done by x-ray in the same manner as the chastised clinic owner on **SIXTY MINUTES**. He was only assuring that the diagnosis would be favorable to the insurance company, which seems only enterprising.

But an x-ray is only two dimensional and I am afraid that best describes the path insurance is forcing dentistry to take.

But maybe I am the one out of step. The insurance companies say they are giving people what they want. Could it be that more and more people care less and less about having a doctor that they know and trust? Many times patients will come in and say "I just want done what the insurance will cover." Our society does seem to be caring less and less about others and growing in self-indulgence. Keep in mind, we can't expect doctors and others who care for us to really care unless there is a quid pro quo. If patients place economics as the highest priority, so will the treating doctors—we are only human.

Another powerful force is the high rate of malpractice claims. We dentists have to practice with a bunker mentality because if conservative treatment involves a measured risk, it may come back to haunt us if the treatment fails. For example, a deep filling that just uncovers the nerve may be treated with a cement capping procedure with a 50/50 chance of preventing a root canal, but many times the patient is upset if in two to three months the capping procedure fails.

There are more frivolous lawsuits filed every day on such failures and many times the insurance company will settle out of court to avoid the court costs. Not long ago a patient refused routine x-rays during a cleaning visit and the hygienist had the patient initial their refusal in the chart. Sometime later, the patient developed a tumor in the jaw and sued the dentist for not finding it. His argument was that he would have had the x-rays if he had known there could be such dire consequences. The court ruled against the dentist.

Recently, a man brought his family into my practice for cleanings and exams. He refused x-rays on any family members, claiming former dentists had always treated them without x-rays. I found myself telling him that we could only clean their teeth but could not even examine them or treat them without x-rays. He left in a huff and I felt terrible because my personal morals of always rendering treatment to someone in need had been violated just to meet the imposed legal dictums.

It is too bad, but every private practitioner I know practices "defensive dentistry" which may not be in the best interest of the patient and may be overly expensive, but it keeps us out of court.

With all this on the minds of clinicians is it any wonder that they fail to listen to our statements about helping their patients by arresting active disease. Many clinicians say it sounds great, but ask me how they can do this and make a living. We are on the cutting edge which is not where a defensive dentist feels comfortable. Most dentists must average between $100 and $150 an hour to keep their offices profitable and they fail to see how the simple procedures we speak of can keep them in the black. It is easier to look for expensive restorative procedures.

Actually, one only needs to look at the typical physician to find the answer. Most physicians in family practice spend the bulk of their time examining healthy patients. There is nothing wrong with providing such a service and there is nothing wrong in making a decent salary doing so. By looking closely at a practice devoted to finding and eliminating your dental diseases, it becomes obvious that this type of dental practice is quite viable and the patients truly the winners. Let's start demanding such quality of service and win together.

# PART TWO
# A PATIENT'S GUIDE TO
# DENTAL HEALTH

# Chapter I
# SELECTING A DENTIST

With all the ways we have to communicate today, it does become confusing as to where to obtain the best advice in selecting a dentist in whom you will have confidence and respect. Each of us has different needs and there is no one "ideal" dentist. But there are some very important guidelines to consider that will greatly aid you in your selection process.

We should start with "improper" reference sources. For example, television commercials advising you to call a central telephone number to receive the name of "the right dentist for you." Be aware that these so-called "independent" information resources are really money-making ventures where doctors are solicited to pay anywhere from $100 to $1000, plus so much for each referral. The only criteria for being on the referral list is paying the fee, although some referral companies do a basic background investigation to ensure their "doctors" have the proper credentials. It is easy to see that the only reason for a physician or a dentist to pay for referrals is an economic one. I don't think many of us place such a reason high on the criteria list for making our selection.

Television and newspaper advertisements are not particularly good sources of information, unless the advertising dentist has a unique procedure that war-

99

rants public attention, ie., to alert the public that they are part of an elite group offering disease management. Since this concept is new and many dentists still do not have a complete understanding as to what it is, such an advertisement may be helpful. Possibly, other procedures such as implants may also fall into this category. If you are in the market for such unique services, these ads should be carefully evaluated.

Calling the local dental society can bring mixed results. These organizations are committed to serve all of their members, and membership only requires a license to practice and the payment of dues. There are some professionals who enjoy the politics of these organizations and become more involved in managing the organization. Often times, these dentists are construed as the finest or best. This may be true but remember that the reputation may have been earned by self-serving political endeavors more than professional skills.

The International Dental Health Foundation inadvertently became a referral service. When articles began appearing in magazines and newspapers about brushing with baking soda and peroxide, etc. , many people began calling and asking for the name of a dentist in their area who practices our treatment methods. We began by giving out the names of professionals who had attended one of our classes. This proved to be unsatisfactory because the professional attended our course but may not have implemented the system. We decided to initiate a membership in the Foundation, the reasoning being that only enthusiastic supporters of the method would want to be members. Members are mailed a quarterly newsletter and an 800-Hotline telephone service is available for advice on individual cases. Many dentists and hygienists have joined over the years and this service is flourishing. As of this writing, we have provided over 35,000 referrals to our member professionals. The interest in our organization also sparked a creation of a membership for non-professionals as many lay people expressed an interest in receiving the newsletter, **ANNOTATIONS**. This has been one of the astonishing successes that keeps our little Foundation going. Although my opinion is obviously biased, I have traveled far and wide throughout this country and had the pleasure of meeting several thousand dentists and hygienists. Those individuals who grasp our ideas and enthusiastically incorporate them into their practices are generally those conscientious professionals who place the welfare of their patients above their own personal gain. I am very proud of our members and truly think that they are the "cream of the crop"—*the finest dentistry has to offer for both disease management and restorative treatment.*

As a bonus for buying this book, I will share with you our toll free number so you may locate the Foundation member closest to you. It is • 800-368-3396.

One final way for you to find a suitable dentist is to ask the opinion of individuals you most respect and trust. Make sure you do not just ask anyone or this method will not work. The reason is that those individuals you respect probably have a vision of the "ideal" dentist similar to yours and, therefore, you will more likely be pleased with the choice. Also, ask this person a variety of questions so you can envision the office yourself before actually calling for an appointment. Ask about personality, the office environment, the staff, and the results of the work performed, and don't forget to ask about the fees.

## Calling For The
## Initial Visit

You will be surprised how great an impression the initial phone call will have and you can use it to your advantage. The person working at the front desk has a very difficult job and may not always be 100% pleasant, but you can tell if she is frantically trying to check patients in and out as well as answer a flurry of phone calls. It is true in a dental office that phone calls seem to come in bunches which is harassing to the reception-ist, but she should still be courteous and show a genuine caring for your needs.

If she seems totally unhurried and wants to sche-dule you with the doctor first for an hour visit for full x-rays, study models, and consultation, you should be aware that this office is probably a low volume, high quality and reasonably expensive practice. They will give lots of attention but somehow they must make their gross income goals. Many people are most comfortable in this kind of setting.

If she can fit you in right away and seemed more interested when you mentioned you were a new pa-tient, this office is obviously looking for new patients. All practitioners start out this way, but after a few years there are so many returning patients that receptionists may lose this eagerness to keep the doctor busy, even though it is constantly mentioned in staff meetings that new patients are high priority and necessary for the vitality of the practice. You may want to inquire how long the doctor has been in practice.

If this is a group practice with more than one doctor, the receptionist more likely will be quite busy. She should be courteous, but quick and walk a fine line between optimum efficiency and rudeness. My office has three doctors and three hygienists and the staff at the front desk are sometimes outright magicians. There are many advantages to group practice. For the patient, it means there will always be a doctor in town to care for your emergencies and the office hours are generally more favorable. Also, the doctors share many overhead expenses so they are in a better position to offer more moderate fees. But you need to be a little more tolerant of their telephone etiquette, at least occasionally.

One last comment—if you wish to select a dentist with a reputation, find out what gave him a reputation. If he is known for his surgery, his treatment plan will emphasize his strengths. If he is known as a crack crown and bridge person, that will be emphasized. Remember to match your needs to the reputation. You don't want to go to a chest surgeon if you have tuberculosis—you might end up short one lung.

# Chapter II
# FIRST VISIT

When you walk into the office your senses will be keen so pay close attention to them. The decor will be a product of the doctor's (or spouse's) taste. If it is not clean or tidy, it means there is a low priority on such matters. The front desk staff should exude a positive, caring attitude and be courteous when escorting you to the examination room.

In my practice, the majority of patients are hard working, middle class, high level federal government or related workers. The Washington scene seems to be a haven for workaholics and many times our patients are on a tight time schedule. They do not want to spend a lot of time in consultation and basically want the bullets—cleaning, efficient exam, explanation of problems and cost, and appointment schedule. For that reason, we schedule new patients with our hygiene staff for one hour. That provides enough time to gather pertinent information, provide an initial cleaning and explain what was found. The only hitch in the system is that the doctor is called in while treating another patient and cannot always spend a large amount of time. If there is active disease or fairly complex repair needed, the patient is rescheduled for a more detailed diagnosis and consultation. X-rays are always required, however, because of the current legal situation and the requirements of insurance companies. If you have previous x-rays, it is necessary to have them on this first visit or the dentist cannot properly evaluate your condition.

What you should be aware of on this initial visit is what all your senses are telling you, both verbally and non-verbally. Ask yourself what is this office's primary interest. Are they more interested in expensive repairs such as crowns, etc., or do they have a genuine interest in your oral health? Do they seem to know about Disease Management as we previously discussed? Are they interested in your disease risk factors and did they discuss the use of a saliva test for the bacteria causing cavities and a microscopic sample for measuring your level of bacteria associated with gum disease? Did they probe gently beneath the gum margin looking for signs of disease and did they carefully look for active decay?

Once the total picture of your needs is examined, the treatment plan should be presented along with the fee. There should be a primary interest in eliminating active disease before going on to repairs. But there are exceptions to this rule as active decay, root canal therapy, or extractions may need to be done immediately. If this is the case, then the immediate repair services are performed simultaneously with Disease Management. Once the diseases are under control the rest of the repairs are scheduled. An example would be that you had a broken tooth. It is wise to build up the broken area with filling material to stabilize the tooth, but a crown is not placed until the gum disease is gone.

Sometimes a tooth is severely compromised and the remaining supporting structures are too weak to keep the tooth stable during normal chewing. If your dentist determines this to be the case, it probably will be necessary to splint the tooth to the adjacent teeth. I generally do this on a temporary basis until the body has a chance to heal the area and regrow bone. Then the splint is removed and the tooth evaluated to see if it can now stand on its own. Sometimes it is necessary to permanently splint the tooth by placing crowns on it and the adjacent teeth. This is only done as a last resort.

## Disease Management
## In The Dental Office

I do not give a caries test to every individual in my practice, although it could be rationalized. Today, many people have conquered decay and their incidence of new disease is practically zero, so I tend to prejudge these individuals knowing full well some would have benefited from the test.

On those individuals that we feel have a decay risk, it is explained and the test offered. The patient has the right to refuse the test and many do, but it is explained that our knowledge of the disease activity is greatly hampered. If the test is given and it comes back positive, we will begin therapy.

The most aggressive treatment is to construct custom plastic trays and instruct the patient how to place a prescription fluoride in the trays and wear them for ten minutes a day, preferably while in the shower. We recommend chewing on the trays which swishes the fluoride in and around the recesses of the tooth structure. If the fluoride comes in contact with decay, it will kill the bacteria and arrest the process. We have had considerable success with the damaged tooth structure remineralizing some of the more open cavities.

For moderate decay problems, diet counseling is of great benefit. Chewing gum is one of the worst habits in our area. Remember, it is the frequency and length of time that sucrose is in the mouth that causes Strep. mutans to attack tooth structure. Sugarless chewing gums with sorbitol can contribute to the problem by growing the bacteria and then, if sucrose follows, it can be most damaging.

Fluorides have many modes of action. They combine with the enamel coating of teeth to make a structure that is less affected by bacterial acids. They do alter the bacteria's ability to function and, if the concentration of fluoride is sufficient, they will actually kill the bacteria.

# Chapter III
# PROFESSIONAL TREATMENT FOR GUM DISEASES

When I first started working with Dr. Keyes, we were not clear on how to put his research information into a busy working environment. I struggled for two years trying various techniques before my results became consistent. Paul and I began traveling together giving lectures, often talking into the wee hours discussing and refining a proper treatment sequence. The outcome was a precise methodology that is taught to clinicians around the country today. The following chapter is an outline of this course as it is taught to dentists and hygienists.

A proper treatment regimen should consist of the following:

• Utilize microbial detection systems to quickly and inexpensively measure the disease activity of patients and assign a risk factor for subsequent disease.

• Identify treatment methods that most effectively eliminate these risk factors starting with the most conservative methods.

• Follow-up treatment procedures to be certain the treatment was successful and the disease eliminated.

• Develop simple preventive systems that will keep patients healthy.

These items were addressed and satisfied when Paul and I created the **Seven Step System for treating periodontal diseases.**

## Step One
## Diagnosis

The first order of business when a patient comes in for routine examination is to determine the level of disease activity and assign a risk factor. The patient's gums are examined with a periodontal probe, a device that allows a clinician to measure the depth of the gum pocket, and it is noted if there is any bleeding and/or swelling. The sites where disease seem most likely are then gently scraped to the base of the pocket and the plaque material is placed on a glass slab to be observed by a phase contrast microscope. Once the slide is scanned, a disease activity risk factor for gum disease is assigned. The caries risk test must be incubated for 48 hours before a treatment plan can be established to correct decay, but the gum disease risk factor can be determined immediately. A treatment plan can be established that details the number of visits and the cost. A simple formula is very helpful in determining the number of visits as explained below:

• The American Dental Association has established guidelines for determining a patient's periodontal **Case Type.** The amount of previous damage is determined by studying x-rays, measuring the pockets, and assessing the bleeding and swelling.There are

Case Types I, II, III, & IV.

• The disease activity risk factor is also calculated and a category of 1, 2, 3 or 4 is assigned.

• By multiplying the Case Type times the Risk Factor and dividing by 2, the approximate number of one hour treatment visits is determined.

• The patient is then assessed for the amount of calculus. This will add or subtract one or two treatment visits.

• Once the number of hours of treatment is known, a proper fee can be assigned by determining all overhead costs per hour and adding 40%. This is multiplied times the number of needed treatment hours. Additional costs for x-rays, microscopic exams, and self-care equipment (irrigators, antiseptics, cannulas, etc. ) are added. The fee should be far less than an estimate for the usual surgical approach.

Our treatment visits involving scaling of the teeth are always at least one hour in length. After active treatment is completed, the visits will be shortened according to the individual case.

Many times in my practice, a patient will be scheduled for a routine cleaning visit and the hygienist will discover active periodontal disease. We save the patient an extra visit and charge for a periodontal exam and consultation by doing an abbreviated cleaning and utilizing the remaining time to gather necessary information to formulate a treatment plan. This is possible since we know we will be scaling the teeth more carefully on future visits.

## Step Two
## Patient Education

It is the patient's right to know what is wrong with his/her oral health and how the dental staff proposes to correct it. The patient then has the latitude to: 1). Accept the treatment, 2). Refuse the treatment. 3). Seek a second opinion. Many times patients from other practices will consult with me for a second opinion. I schedule such visits for one hour. With my staff's help, all pertinent information is gathered and these patients are given a full explanation of our view of their periodontal disease situation including: 1). The nature of their condition, 2). The detailed treatment plan, 3). Risks, 4). Alternatives, 5). Possible complications. These five items are considered *Informed Consent*, which is recognized in a law court as the patients' legal rights. On second opinion visits generally no treatment is rendered, as the patient should have the right to go home, ponder what has been told to them and then decide who will provide treatment.

When complicated restorative procedures, such as crowns and bridges, are involved, the patient has a right to know not only the risks and complications of the treatment, but the risks and complications of no treatment.

Since there are many misconceptions and controversies about periodontal treatment, I generally offer the patient background information on the history of dental diseases and problems that evolved in their management. The same is true for decay. For example, it is entirely conceivable to treat many decayed lesions with fluoride treatments. This is totally unheard of in most dental practices.

## Sample Treatment Plan

Risk Factor = 3
Case Type = 3
Add for calculus = 1
10/2 = 5 treatment visits (4, 1 hr)( 1, 1/2 hr)

Cost of treatment would be 4.5 hours times overhead plus 40%, plus microscopic slides, irrigators, x-rays, etc.

## Typical Treatment Plans

### Beginning disease

One scaling visit, one follow-up assessment, recall in three to four months, then assess for longer periods between maintenance visits.

### Moderate disease

Two or three scaling visits, one or two follow-up assessments, then maintenance is established.

### Advanced disease

Four to six scaling visits, two assessments, then establish maintenance. Generally, since a fair amount of damage has occurred to the bone structure, the period between maintenance visits is kept at about three months.

## Very advanced disease
## with threatening tooth loss

Five to eight scaling visits, two assessments, then establish maintenance. Since the teeth and supporting structures are severely compromised, it is advisable for this patient to be evaluated during maintenance at two to three month intervals.

There are other complicating factors that might need to be included in the treatment plan. Most common is an evaluation and adjustment of the way the teeth bite together. For example, if one tooth hits the opposite tooth before other teeth meet, it will place undue stress on that tooth's supporting structures and enhance destruction. Adjustment of the bite is necessary to promote healing. Sometimes patients may grind their teeth which, also, places undue stress on the supporting tissues. This can be alleviated with a bite splint and/or bite adjustment by carefully removing part of the tooth that is hitting too hard.

Sometimes there are complex restorative problems that must be solved simultaneously with periodontal treatment. This could involve splinting together two or more teeth, root canal treatments, etc.

It is also necessary to evaluate the patient's general health as many other diseases will affect the dental treatment plan. When a patient is in treatment for other problems, the physician's treatment could easily alter the dentist's treatment. A patient should inform the dentist of any medical problems or other treatments.

## Step Three
## Treatment

Our philosophy of treatment is that we should attempt the simplest, least invasive procedures that might succeed initially, then modify the therapy. Since we have been successful in treating non-surgically even the most advanced case—many of which had endured previous surgery or been considered hopeless by periodontists or other dental professionals—we **never** recommend surgery during the first six months of therapy.

Scaling and root planing have been found to be necessary, at least with today's methods, to break up thick mats of bacteria and to remove most of the accumulated tartar or calculus. No matter what technique has been used (surgical or non-surgical) all calculus will not be removed. Our work has shown that such removal is not necessary if the calculus is thin enough and can be sterilized by repeated irrigations. There are many periodontists who believe that not only must plaque and calculus be removed, but, also, the outer layer of the root surface. They point to studies showing bacteria in the small tubules of this layer as evidence. I strongly disagree. Research performed at the microbiology laboratory at University of Michigan has shown that bacteria can exist deep into the root structure, so it is impossible to scrape all bacteria away. Besides, it has been my experience that we can eliminate these bacteria in almost all cases with repeated irrigations over a long period of time. That is why it takes months of irrigations to reach a "cure". The side effects suffered by removal of the root surface are also to be considered. Sensitivity is experienced universally by patients that have been so vigorously root planed and the roots are far more prone to decay. If a particular area of the mouth has not responded to our treatment after several months, such vigorous root planing could be of some value and would be considered at that time.

Another procedure recommended by dental clinicians is curettage. This is really a surgical procedure performed because bacteria have been found to penetrate the inner lining of gum tissue. Also this tissue has been altered by the body to deal with the bacteria and is lumpy, engorged with blood vessels, and referred to as granular tissue. I strongly disagree with the removal of this tissue because it possesses those tissue cells that perform healing. My experience has been that such tissue actually aids in healing. If, after several months, I think that healing has not occurred, I will consider removing this tissue and allowing the body to form fresh tissue that may contain more healing cells. Rarely do I need to resort to cementum removal or curettage.

Generally, we do a simple root planing procedure and try not to scrape away the root surface. If there is a fair amount of calculus, I like to have one visit devoted to removing the heavy layers of calculus. Then, if it is an advanced case, the mouth is divided into four quadrants and the patient is given local anesthesia. Since it often requires an hour to properly root plane one quadrant, the patient will need four visits to complete the root planing procedure.

Our treatment steps would be:
1. Assess the current disease activity microscopically.
2. Assess the patient's Home Care regimen.
3. Measure pockets as indicated
4. Irrigate thoroughly with a powerful antiseptic.
5. Meticulously root plane and scale to the depths of all the pockets.
6. Irrigate thoroughly again.
7. Review and modulate home care as needed.
8. Establish next appointment.

There is evidence that ultrasonic devices are superior to hand scaling instruments. However, these instruments have been designed to only remove calculus above the gum line. Recent experiments reveal that specially designed instrument tips allow access to the areas below the gum and do a better job of getting in between the roots of multi-rooted teeth. I am greatly encouraged by these findings and predict that such instruments will be the standard in a few years.

## Step Four
## Patient Education

Since the patient has the opportunity to treat one's self everyday, self treatment is the most important part of the whole process. Consistently repeated treatment measures are bound to have the greatest success. The problem then becomes one of properly instructing the patient and following through to make certain the patient is doing what is required. This sounds so easy, but in reality it is the hardest part. Most patients are somewhat intimidated when a hygienist or dentist is telling them how to take care of their teeth. They are much more interested when they learn their problem is the fault of the germs they have observed on the television monitor and not just the result of careless brushing.

But it also takes a bit of understanding and perseverance for most people to change their daily habits. If a person knows that someone else really cares about the health of their teeth and supports them during the learning process when clumsiness reigns, change in habits *will* occur. We clinicians need to hone our skills in this area so learning self-care becomes fashionable, acceptable and easily attainable. I allow about twenty minutes at the end of the first scaling visit to go over the self-care steps carefully. At the beginning of subsequent visits, I evaluate how well the patient is doing. If we are using a powerful antimicrobial agent that we know kills our bacterial targets and a proper delivery system, then the only variable is how well the patient is performing. If areas of subgingival plaque remain, a sample is removed and observed under the microscope. It becomes immediately obvious if this area has been missed regularly, occasionally or recently. Generally, what happens is that a few areas around the most posterior teeth are missed and we zero in on these areas with the patient watching. We actually guide the patient's own hands to deliver the antiseptic to the missed area.

Each office visit we aid the patient in refining home care techniques until the disease is gone. Psychologists call this type of behavior modification "shaping". It is most effective and patients are never chastised for lack of motivation or ability. After all, it is their mouth and my job is only to aid them in staying healthy. I usually make the comment that it is their battle with the disease; my job is to direct the winning strategy. If they are aggressive and motivated to do a meticulous job everyday, my involvement is reduced and they will be rewarded with fewer appointments. If they are underachievers, they will see me more often.

## Home Care For Beginning Gum Disease

In this case, the home care instructions are very simple. Usually the pockets are shallow and normal brushing with a proper stroke will reach to the depths of the pockets. Therefore, the patient can use Baking Soda, Dental Care toothpaste or Viadent toothpaste as a dentifrice and eliminate the infection. We like to follow up in about eight weeks to be certain what we prescribed worked. If it did not, then a Viadent irrigator with a sulcus tip and an irrigating agent such as, Viadent Rinse, Salt Water, Vinegar (diluted), etc. will be added.

## Home Care For Moderate Gum Disease

Since the majority of patients fall into this category, it is an area of great concern in our practice. The patient must be aware that he/she is on the verge of major problems that could lead to tooth loss if the bone degeneration continues. We stress the use of the irrigator, both the Water Pik with its PIKPOCKET delivery tips and the Viadent with its SULCUS TIP. Both are adequate for the job. Stronger antimicrobial irrigation solutions are prescribed, such as; agents with chlorhexidine .02%, Stannous Fluoride, Saturated Salt Water, Chloramine T, etc. The current Viadent Rinse is the best of the over-the-counter mouthrinses, but sometimes it is too weak to be completely effective for this case. Some of my patients use Listerine, which does not seem to be completely effective against our subgingival bacterial targets and they probably will need to switch off to different agents used on alternating days.

I prefer to prescribe brushing with a baking soda and peroxide paste (one teaspoonful baking soda to one-half capful peroxide) for a short while, as this combination is a much stronger dentifrice than anything else and works very well. After a few months, we generally switch to either Dental Care or Viadent. Peroxide is a powerful antibacterial agent by itself and I have used it as an irrigating agent in the past. If this is done, it should be diluted to 1 1/2% and only used for a short period of time. Chronic use will greatly alter the entire bacterial flora and cause changes in the tissue cells. The small amount in the Baking Soda/ Peroxide mixture does not cause such massive bacterial destruction and, therefore, can be used for longer periods of time.

### Home Care for Advanced Gum Disease

When the gum pockets become deeper than five millimeters (about the same as 1/4 inch), the case is considered advanced. Almost half of the entire bone supporting a tooth is gone and bone loss must be stopped and, hopefully, reversed or tooth loss will occur in the near future.

Daily irrigation at home becomes mandatory and the more powerful agents would be employed, such as chlorhexidine and chloramine T. I have found that a dilute solution of chlorox is also of some help. *PLEASE* realize that this is a very dilute solution measured by mixing 1/2 capful from a quart bottle of chlorox (this is about one part chlorox to sixty parts water) with a full reservoir of warm water in the irrigator. This is recommended only for a short period of time to bring the bacterial counts down to more manageable levels. Chloramine T and chlorhexidine are only available by prescription and must be used under a dentist's care. Saturated warm salt water has also been effective. I would strongly recommend the use of any agent only under the direct supervision of your dentist. If burning or discomfort is experienced, the solutions should be discontinued and your dentist consulted.

In order to reach the depths of these advanced areas, it is necessary to use a cannula device. A cannula looks like a needle used for blowing up a football, basketball, or soccerball. The gauge of the cannula is large and the end is round with the hole coming out about a millimeter above the end. It fits on a connector that slides into the Viajet irrigator. The cannulas and connector must be purchased through a dentist.

After the patient has irrigated, it is recommended

that they brush with a mixture of baking soda and peroxide to kill remaining germ life. It will also remove the aftertaste from the antiseptic. If the patient rinses thoroughly with warm water immediately after brushing, the effects from sodium on blood pressure are greatly minimized.

Sometimes these patients experience sensitivity due to the exposure of root surfaces after the bone tissue is lost. Sensitivity can be alleviated by using a prescription grade fluoride gel as toothpaste once a day. In severe cases, a plastic mouthpiece (looks like a football mouthguard) is constructed and the gel is placed in the mouthpiece and worn for ten minutes a day.

### Home Care For The Very
### Advanced Periodontal Case

These cases are so individualized that it is impossible to describe generally what is done. Such advanced patients will be using an irrigator with cannulas in my practice, as this is the best tool a patient can use. The solutions vary and sometimes I will prescribe two or three different irrigation solutions to be used on alternate days. Patients are seen frequently to refine their home care and to closely monitor the progress. Most of these cases will require at least one course of antibiotics. It would be hard to imagine any patient being able to conquer their disease all by themselves when it is advanced and supervision by a dentist who is trained and interested in disease management is really needed. In the event that no dentist is available, I would try to obtain an irrigator with either the PIK-POCKETS or SULCUS TIPS and irrigate with concentrated warm salt water. If you cannot have salt for medical reasons, try the chlorox and alternate with vinegar diluted 50/50 with water.

### Step Five
### Monitoring The Progress

This has really been discussed in previous steps, but we made it a separate step to emphasize its importance. There is no way anyone can do an effective job of treating bacterial infections without monitoring the bacteria. Many of my colleagues will do some version of the first four steps and jump directly to maintenance. Over half of all cases do not respond exactly as planned and some form of change in the treatment plan is called for. This means that those who do not properly monitor the bacteria will suffer failure in over half of their cases. With all we know today, our patients *deserve better than that.* I still am a fervent believer that the phase-contrast microscope does this job better than anything else available on the market and allows us the opportunity to sort out which patient needs revisions in his or her treatment. Besides identifying the disease associated bacteria, such monitoring tells whether the antiseptics are reaching the bacteria, as we know the potential of our agents. This is a quality control measure to ensure the success of our treatment plans. When bacteria are still present, then STEP SIX is necessary.

## Step Six
## Modulation Of Therapy

A 1981 research article pointed out that the five-year success rate for currently offered "conventional" periodontal therapy is only about twenty-seven per cent. The criteria for determining unsuccessful treatment was renewed bone loss. We are experiencing a far better success rate than that. Although we do not have precise hard data at this time, we expect ninety per cent of our treated cases not to suffer renewed bone loss five years after treatment. Let's take a hard look at the cases that do not respond initially and have that potential to recur.

When disease continues in spite of treatment the health professions use the term "refractory case." This term has not been well defined and clinicians have different meanings. For our purposes, let us assume that when the treatment phase is completed and our end points have not been reached, such a lack of cure could be divided into three distinct categories:

1. *AT RISK*—Those cases which have not actually demonstrated renewed bone loss, but still exhibit bacteria associated with disease. Such a category has not yet been recognized by other dental organizations, but is frequently a problem for our Foundation member clinicians—twenty to thirty per cent of all cases. Generally, the bacteria are not in high numbers and the white blood cells are in the two plus category. Clinically, the infection seems minimal with few or no clinical signs such as, bleeding upon probing, soft tissue swelling, or loss of attachment.

2. *RECALCITRANT*—Cases that respond to therapy and the disease-associated bacteria are not detected at the end of treatment phase, but tend to return during maintenance. These patients can be managed without further bone loss if the frequency of patient visits is properly adjusted to the individual needs of that patient. These cases seem to occur in approximately twenty per cent of cases treated.

3. *REFRACTORY*—Cases that do not respond to active therapy. Fortunately, these cases are rare (less than five per cent), but are extremely taxing and generate the most concern as the patient is suffering continued loss of bone. In our favor, however, the activity seems to be confined to one or only a few teeth.

In general, all three conditions require a modulation of therapy and the clinician must establish a protocol system to determine which modulation is right for each individual case.

The following is a list of possible causes and solutions that a treating dentist or hygienist might follow, starting with the most likely to the least likely possibilities:

(1) The antimicrobial agent is not reaching the site of the infection:

> a) Patient not properly performing self treatment measures. Solution: Check method of delivery and retrain the patient. Check at three week intervals until successful. It may be necessary to schedule the patient for frequent professional irrigations. It must be remembered that even strong antiseptics do

not penetrate thick bacterial mats completely, thus such agents must be used in conjunction with meticulous root planing.

b) Calculus remains that harbors a bacterial mat too thick for agents to penetrate. Solution: Repeat root planing in the target areas followed by professional irrigation. Observe at three week intervals until successful. Antibiotics may be necessary.

c) The body has not resolved granulomatous soft tissue that provides a harbor for disease associated bacteria. Solution: Perform granulomatous soft tissue curettage and irrigate extensively. Sometimes malocclusion contributes by constantly traumatizing the involved teeth. Carefully screen all jaw movements for premature contacts and determine if temporary splinting is needed. Check in three weeks.

d) Delivery system is wrong for the case. Switch to at-home irrigation with rounded 24 gauge cannulas. In some cases the PIK POCKET or sulcus tip may work.

(2) The selected antimicrobial agent is not completely effective. Reasons include:

a) Some agents do not work well in the presence of bleeding. This is true of most oxidizing agents, such as chlorhexidine, etc.

b) Improper selection of agent — try stronger agent.

c) Agent not used at the proper concentration

—check patient's mixing techniques.
d) Bacteria are resistant to agent (rare)—change agent.

(3) Re-infection from an outside source (another individual). Such a problem seems most prevalent in Recalcitrant cases. Patient counseling and treatment of the outside source are highly recommended. It is most helpful to give both parties a course of antibiotics simultaneously.

(4) Host resistance factors that allow bacteria associated with disease to penetrate body tissues, thus establishing "reservoirs" of bacteria that seem untouched by aggressive treatment. This is suspected in true refractory cases. Spirochetes and motile rods have been found in tooth dentine tubules and connective tissues away from the actual infected zone. Contributing factors may include deficiencies in the way a person's body reacts to the bacteria, such as: white blood cell deficiency and other immunological disorders. Systemic disease including: diabetes, anemia, blood dyscrasia, and degenerative connective tissue diseases may be involved. My observation has been that when these factors contribute the numbers of white blood cells remain high. Many times the clinical signs are negative and the tissues appear normal.

(5) Abnormal pathogens: This occurs in very few cases and is generally a gram positive non-motile organism and responds quite well to Amoxicillin or Keflex antibiotics.

(6) Compromised supporting tissues: In very advanced periodontal disease it is possible that even normal biting forces injure the remaining supporting bone and attached tissues. This is the case when there is persistent mobility and inflammation. Splinting and certain surgical procedures should be considered.

(7) Reinfection of an unresolved pocket: Pockets that heal to 4mm depths or better are easily maintained. Deeper pockets that are closely adapted to the root surface will do well if only irrigation procedures are continued through maintenance at least twice a week. The maintenance interval should be individualized for each patient.

If the tissue around deeper pockets is incomplete or loosely positioned, bacteria-laden debris can be constantly forced into the pocket. Such a condition requires meticulous care by the patient and surgical recontouring should be discussed with the patient.

Out of the thousands of cases observed only a handful presented totally baffling refractory problems. One such case was examined by two universities in 1975-77. Diagnosis was rapidly advancing periodontal disease with poor prognosis. The patient's mother had lost her teeth in her early thirties and the patient was now the same age. Proposed treatment was ten extractions and flap surgery, then partial dentures. The patient opted for Dr. Paul Keyes' study at the National Institutes of Health. Dr. Keyes treated him until 1980 when the study was completed and the patient came to my practice. Although, as of this writing, he has not lost a tooth, he has experienced acute episodes of recurrence. On his visit of June 22,1988, he reported a recent abscess. Microscopy revealed the smallest species of spirochetes and spinning rods. Definite bone loss had occurred around his upper left molar. This happened despite daily irrigation and close observation plus aggressive professional treatment. Over the course of the eight years I have treated him, we have found it necessary to prescribe ten courses of antibiotics. He is single and claims no oral contact with anyone in the last year.

Conclusion is that he "harbors a reservoir" or residuum infection somewhere that may be distant from the periodontal area and is not touched by the antibiotic. This reservoir continues to re-infect the periodontal pockets. At least we expect tooth loss to be minimal.

Thank goodness such cases are rare, but we all need to be aware of their existence.

### Step Seven
### Maintenance

Once the targeted bacteria are eliminated and the pockets have shown signs of healing, the patient is considered out of the treatment phase and in the maintenance phase. The strategy here is different as our goal is to prevent any new infections.

We attempt to individualize the periods between office visits to meet each patient's needs. As a rule, the more previous destruction the less time between visits. The most advanced cases are placed on two month recalls, while the beginning disease cases can go up to a year. Each time a patient comes in, we review the home-care procedures trying to make the self care treatment time as efficient as possible.

The length of time between recall visits is adjusted at each appointment. If a patient is making excellent progress, he/she is rewarded by lengthening the recall time. If a patient has slipped and shows disease activity we make an appointment for treatment and shorten the recall time until the patient demonstrates the ability to maintain health.

# Chapter IV
# WHERE DO WE GO FROM HERE?

Recently, a colleague who is a periodontist related an experience that he had the previous week. He was invited to participate in a focus group, where he and four other periodontists were asked a series of questions. The five periodontists had been selected at random by an unknown company and brought together to discuss topics on which the company wanted their "expert" opinion. The colleague was appalled to learn that none of the other four periodontists knew that gum diseases were definitely bacterial infections. He was further amazed when he challenged them, citing various articles from journals, that two of them were not even aware of the existence of one of the most renown international periodontal research journals.

It was most discouraging to me after I had given an eight-hour lecture to a group of dentists and one of the participants had come up to me and said "I really appreciated the lecture but it really isn't for me. My most pressing problem at this time is my back hand". Pat Cartwright and I have often lamented about the lack of interest by the majority of the profession. We thought that, since there has been a preponderance of research in the last few years supporting an antimicro-

131

bial approach, the interest level would have increased. We launched a major educational effort with seminars for dental personnel in several cities and a symposium featuring some of the world's most outstanding researchers. Our response has been mostly from those individuals who have taken previous courses, so over eighty per cent of the profession are just not interested. Paul Keyes has said for the last six years that he held no hope for the dental profession solving the disease problem. He still feels that dental diseases will be eradicated from forces outside the profession. He points to the fact that the addition of fluoride to drinking water has provided the single most important factor in lowering the incidence of caries. This really occurred not through the efforts of the dental profession, but certain researchers and the government.

At well known universities considered by many to be the best dental schools in the country, dental researchers have run into insurmountable obstacles with the schools' administrators and have managed to continue their pioneering research only with support from the medical schools. Medicine has shown more than a passing interest in dental research's sophisticated techniques for growing anaerobic bacteria. They probably recognize that many respiratory infections could be from this family of bacteria and, by altering the bacterial flora in the various parts of the gastrointestinal tract, we may be able to greatly improve health. Conditions like chronic sinus infections and bronchitis may be explained and eliminated. Other stomach disorders and colon inflammations, along with certain cancers, may be eliminated.

Medicine is also beginning to look for more things to do as the population of physicians increases. It may be that Ear, Nose and Throat (ENT) doctors will be interested in treating the oral or dental infections. Certainly one does not need a dental license to treat bacterial infections of the mouth and people just may prefer to be treated in the hands of these physicians. It may be exactly what happens unless dentistry makes a sudden about face in the very near future. Let's look at some possible changes in dental education.

Dental schools should consider changing their curriculum to allow more emphasis on the management of oral infections and less on some of the lesser used restorative procedures. This could happen easily because methods and materials for restoring teeth have advanced to the point that many complex, time consuming procedures could be dropped from the D.D.S. curriculum. For example, there are fewer and fewer people that require dentures and making them could be incorporated into graduate programs, so the making of dentures would be provided by prosthodontists. The time in undergraduate programs would then be allocated to disease management.

A real crisis is looming in the dental hygiene area. The great demand for hygienists is causing competition among dental practices and hygienists are demanding higher and higher salaries. In the Washington D.C. area a hygienist can graduate from a two year program and be offered between $20 and $30 an hour to come to work in over a dozen different offices. Near-sighted hygienists are constantly looking for the highest salary and do not hesitate leaving one practice

for another. Local groups of dentists are mounting
efforts to influence Virginia lawmakers to change the
dental hygiene licensing procedures and make it possible for a dentist to train dental assistants for a two-
week period in selected practices to receive a dental
hygiene license. Under such a training program, there
would be no incentive for a hygienist to receive a
formal education and hygiene would become a trade at
a time when the American public needs a hygiene
profession.

Making hygiene a profession would be the easiest
and most efficient way to bring about an economical
dental disease management program. Most dentists
view disease management as a hygiene or cleaning
problem which is most certainly below a dentist's level
of training and they simply are not interested in doing
it. Because of this attitude, there would probably be
less resistance to changing hygienists' courses than
dental school courses.

The largest hurdle is allowing the dental hygienists to have more responsibility. Most dentists, when
dealing with the issue through organized societies, feel
that the two year hygiene program is really a vocation-
al school and graduates need the direct supervision of
dentists. On the other hand, hygienists have been
struggling to become professionals and many programs have been upgraded to include one or two years
of liberal arts leading to a bachelor's degree. Many
contend that they should be considered professionals
with a right to practice independently. They argue
that people should be able to get their teeth cleaned by
an independent operator that could refer all needed

dentistry to practicing dentists. Organized dentistry dimly views this position as undermining the authority of dentists to diagnose and refer. They know that hygiene visits have been a profit center and a constant source of business as necessary dental work is picked up during the regularly scheduled recall visit to their office. Having to rely on referrals by an independent hygienist is vigorously opposed, although the hygienists are often strapped with the responsibility of diagnosing and "selling" dental work for the benefit of the dental practice and performing whatever disease management that is done in their employer's practice.

I see that hygiene programs could be enhanced by making the program at least four academic years and adding necessary courses to create a professional capable of managing oral diseases. They could provide both caries and periodontal management, referring those patients that did not respond to treatment within a prescribed period of time to the general dentists or periodontists. This would provide ample patients to keep the periodontists busy and by referring restorative work to general dentists they should be relatively content. There would be a need for relatively small number of general dentists to aid in training and directing this new profession. Since about five per cent of the dentists have become members of our Foundation and are enthusiastically practicing good disease management, this would be an excellent source to find these dental educators.

The new professional degree could be called a Bachelor of Science in Oral Disease Therapy and the graduate could practice within the confines of a general dental office or independently. Actually, I envision a dental disease management clinic with one dentist diagnosing and prescribing treatment with ten to twelve therapists providing the actual work. Once again, the five per cent of the general dentists who have trained themselves to manage oral diseases could provide such a function. Oral diseases would be quickly eliminated from the patients of such a clinic and then they would be provided with constant preventive therapy. The numbers of restorative procedures necessary would dwindle as the patient would encounter little or no damage from new disease. The bottom line would be less costs with healthier mouths.

We are at a major crossroads. If the hygiene program becomes a trade, the public will suffer dental diseases for many more years. If a Bachelor of Oral Disease Therapy program is established, the incidence of dental diseases will diminish almost immediately. I only wish a philanthropist would help underwrite establishment of such a school. The Therapist would receive a respectable income and, since they are given the authority to manage their own patients, there will be an increased interest by students to seek a career in Oral Disease Therapy.

In order to provide incentives for the success of such a program, some fundamental changes should be made in dental insurance. Right now the only reason to have dental insurance is to figure out how to get someone else to pay for your problems. It is most attractive to a person who needs a fair amount of work and wants his company or other members of the insured group to foot the bill. Insurance companies spend their time creating fine print to limit their exposure while keeping insurance packages competitive and attractive. The companies either make their thirty to forty per cent or they get out of the business and concentrate on a more profitable area of insurance. Most companies have watched their dental benefits packages creep upward in cost and now are faced with reducing or eliminating the benefit. Here is an alternative:

### Three, Two, One
### Capitation Plan

Members of a group or a business join the Plan with the idea that initial costs are higher and then decrease as the patients become healthier. For example, the first year each member could be assessed $300, with the first $100 paid by the company. At the end of the first year, if the member becomes healthier with fewer restorative needs and the risk of new disease decreases, they would be rewarded with less costs—say $200 per year with the company still picking up the first $100. Then at the end of the second year, if the patient still showed minimal risk, the cost would be lowered to $100 per year. This places the burden of health to the person insured and would work provided the dental clinic doing the work understood disease management (A great place for an Oral Disease Therapist).

The best way to establish such a program would be under a Preferred Provider Package where private practices would be encouraged to join the capitation program. The International Dental Health Foundation would be willing to work on this problem if there was sufficient interest.

## Direct Care

The most cost effective way to produce dental care is for companies to establish their own clinics. There are many ways to make this program effective. One way would be for the employee to pick up a certain percentage of the cost. This amount could be lowered by seniority and disease risk. Everyone wins with this type of program provided there is a peer review process to ensure the quality of service provided. Again, IDHF could aid in this process. Obviously, a large organization is needed to afford an in-house clinic, but a similar arrangement could be possible through a local Chamber of Commerce with the Chamber contracting with the professionals.

## Employee Payroll
## Deduction Plan

This is an interesting concept where the company pays the cost for disease management and diagnosis. Then a note is sent to the company with the estimate of the cost of the treatment necessary. The company deducts the amount over a prescribed period of time and sends it to the dental practice. Work progresses immediately and is completed in a reasonable amount of time. The dental practice agrees to do the work for seventy-five per cent of usual and customary fees that are reviewed on an annual basis. The added benefit of this plan is that the dental bill is deducted before taxes and the practice benefits by having payment up front. The only requirement is for the company and the selected dental practice to develop a bookkeeping system. I see this type of plan as perfect to be managed by a Chamber of Commerce so smaller businesses can participate. The only drawback is that the dental practices would need to be group practices so they could provide care for the numbers necessary. Once again, the employee would need to chose one of the dentists practicing within that group practice. But the benefit gained is tremendous and seems to be the fairest method of meeting the demand for care and maintaining adequate income for those clinicians providing the service

Details for all three concepts could be worked out by the International Dental Health Foundation which could serve as a peer review and mediator. Anyone interested should contact the Foundation by writing to IDHF, 11484 Washington Plaza West, Reston, VA 22090.

## New Dental Care Agents For Home Care

Probably this is the most exciting area in dentistry. When you stop to think about the fact that we have relied on a bristle brush to control dental diseases with only marginal success, it is time that we applied modern thinking to the problem and come up with far better home-care methods.

There are many new agents currently being tested to meet FDA standards and some of these should be available in the very near future. ViPont Corporation is developing a new prescription grade substance utilizing their active ingredient *Sanguinarine*. The substance is being incorporated into a biodegradable polymer that can be injected below the gumline where it hardens and slowly dissolves, thus providing a constant delivery of an antimicrobial agent. *Sanguinarine* has been shown to have favorable effect on the bacteria associated with dental diseases. If it meets all expectations, a patient needs only to go into a dental clinic and receive the injections once every few months and no disease will occur *no matter whether the person brushes their his/her teeth everyday or not.*

**Oral B Corporation** is developing a simple detection system to screen large numbers of people for gum disease. They are also developing a timed release system similar to the ViPont system that allows a small amount of the antibiotic, **Metronidazole**, to be released. This will be extremely helpful in treating the millions of people with existing gum disease. Both of these agents will also be effective in lowering decay so all dental diseases will be easily eliminated.

I cannot wait to arrive in China or other third world countries with a boatload of these agents and tools and train nurses and other assistants to deliver the agents to the masses of people that have suffered all their lives with mouth pain. I also have some other ideas for products that could make dental diseases only memories in a short period of time with minimum cost.

This is a most exciting time to be a part of the dental profession but also is frustrating due to resistance to change. Therefore, it is up to you, the public, to demand these changes and together we can make it happen.

## What Can You Do
## Right Now?

First of all, you need to know what to do for yourselves. You can find out the nearest dentist to you that has taken courses offered by the Foundation by writing IDHF and getting a list of the professional members in your state. Next you could become a lay member of the Foundation for a nominal $20 a year fee and receive a quarterly issue of the Newsletter *ANNO-TATIONS*. In this way you can keep informed on the latest products, changes in the dental profession, and new research that impacts on our system of treatment.

If there is no understanding dentist near you, the following self treatment would be of benefit although professional help is strongly recommended:

If you are under 35 and have never experienced problems with decay, bleeding gums or never been told by a dental professional that you have any gum problems, you probably can best benefit from a simple preventive program. That could consist of no more than regular brushing with Dental Care toothpaste by Arm & Hammer or using the Viadent system. Viadent recommends regular brushing with their toothpaste and rinsing for up to a minute twice a day with Viadent rinse. Since there is a definite cumulative effect from the rinsing, the recommended regimen that comes with the rinse should be followed carefully. Studies that seem to find fault with proclaimed benefits from Viadent generally do not properly follow the recommended regimen, so using it correctly is critical. I personally like the Dental Care because it doesn't cake the bristles of the toothbrush, but many people object to the sweetness and the saltiness of Dental Care. Either product is far and away better than any other product on the market as others do not include antimicrobial, agents and, therefore, will not prevent you from getting decay and gum disease. It is also wise to floss at least two or three times a week.

Many of you, however, know that your gum tissues occasionally bleed when brushed and sometimes feel strange—like an itchy pain. Others have noticed soreness while flossing and/or some bleeding. This means that you cannot use just a simple preventive system and need additional care. The simplest system involves the use of the irrigator. I currently use the ViaJet irrigator as it is inexpensive and has the highest quality of all irrigators currently available. Water Pik would be a second choice. The advantage of an irrigator is that it will direct a stream of antimicrobial agent down under the gums where brushing will not reach. I would recommend that you brush with Baking Soda and Peroxide for a month or two as these agents are much more potent than Dental Care and Viadent. Just wet your toothbrush in Peroxide and dip it into the Baking Soda. The powder will stick to your brush and you can commence brushing. If it is easier, you can make a paste with a 1/2 capful of Peroxide and a teaspoon of Baking Soda. Using this mixture for a short time and following up with an irrigation could possibly relieve your gum problems and prevent decay provided you do not frequently eat foods containing high amounts of sugar and none of your gum pockets are so deep that simple irrigation did not penetrate far enough. It is advisable to continue flossing at least twice a week.

If you know that you have definite gum problems or you are aware of holes in your teeth, it is advisable to seek help from a dental professional. When this is not possible, consider using the ViaJet irrigator with the clear sulcus tip or the Water Pik with the Pik Pockets. These delivery tips will allow you to direct the stream deeper into the gums and by using stronger antimicrobial agents you may successfully arrest your disease. The most effective agent against decay is fluoride, so you could direct one of the commercial fluoride solutions around your teeth and into the holes. This can actually stop the decay process. With gum disease, you will need to use some very strong agents. I would recommend a saturated very warm salt solution directed through the Sulcus Tip or the Pik Pocket down into the gum pockets as deep as possible. If salt water is not possible, use the very weak chlorox (1/2 capful to a full irrigator reservoir of warm water). This can only be used for a very short period of time.

There are prescription grade agents that are only available from a dentist. For serious decay problems, I always prescribe a strong fluoride gel for toothbrushing. Actually, after dipping the toothbrush in Peroxide, apply a fluoride gel to the brush and brush the teeth for an extremely clean feeling.

Many alternative agents are effective but there are no research data to back up their safety. It is highly recommended that you find a dentist or hygienist who have the proper training, use a microscope and know what to do to eliminate your particular disease.

If you have a regular dentist that you trust and feel confident he/she is providing you optimum care, don't be hasty to change. Such a relationship is precious so, first, try to encourage him/her to seek continuing education training in disease management. There are many honest, hard-working dentists who are just too consumed with other parts of dentistry and haven't even thought about treating infection.

Next you can encourage your employer to seek out one of the insurance programs discussed in this book or at least try to influence your company's insurance company to embrace disease management.

Lastly you could encourage your company to support the Foundation's efforts. We exist only with a clear cut purpose to end dental diseases as soon as possible. This kind of effort takes funds and with such funds the International Dental Health Foundation could:

1. direct proper research.
2. help develop new products.
3. start a new dental education program.
4. direct new dental insurance programs.
5. bring information to the American people.

If you have found a dentist in whom you have the utmost confidence, you are fortunate. Just bear in mind that this dentist is right for you no matter whether your insurance covers his charges or not. Insurances have designed their coverage based solely on economic reasons and your dentist is trying to give you the best care for your particular needs. Sometimes such cross purposes are not compatible. Yes, it is more expensive to stick with one dentist no matter what the problem, but you will be receiving true professional care. I believe that many dentists truly want to provide optimum care as he or she sees it. But much of dentistry is still an art and, therefore, there are many ways to treat similar problems and your dentist may opt for treatment that is different than someone else.

If you believe in that dentist, then he is probably providing you with the type of restorative treatment you want and any reasonable free is justified. A dentist has to compromise when a patient only wants what his/her insurance will cover.

One area, however, that is out of balance in most practices is disease management. You deserve to know if you are at risk of dental diseases and you deserve to have the option to treatment before your teeth are damaged.

The prevailing thought in the dental profession is that the bacteria associated with all dental diseases is in almost every mouth, so the only course of action is to reduce their numbers. This has validity since such reduction has resulted in less destruction, so hygiene measures are relied upon.

The problem is that prevention is often confused with treatment. No doubt, medicine has found that hygiene of the skin, ie. daily showers, has reduced many skin infections, such as boils and impetigo. But once such diseases appear, medicine promotes treatment that eliminates offending bacteria. We need to do the same in dentistry. Besides, dental hygiene measures have not been that effective. If they were, we would not have the incidence of disease that currently exists.

Research of American Indian tribes revealed that those Indians who did not seek regular dental care had far more teeth than those regularly visiting public clinics. One could argue that the extractions alleviated pain and suffering, but would we accept the removal of fingers to alleviate the pain of athritis? We should demand better ways to save teeth as such ways exist. Demand it!

Let members of the dental profession not argue about how dental diseases have been treated in the past, or to protect self interests, but use the knowledge available to end this suffering once and for all.